(*continued from front flap*)

which attempts to found a human paradise on Earth. This is shown to be an illusion in the face of a real spiritual universe based on God's love and justice.

The last part of this volume is a vivid description of future spiritual life. Hell is described in all its horror and awesomeness— its reality is brought back into a focus from which many modern Christians had allowed it to slip. Hell, it is pointed out, is as real as Heaven.

This is an important volume for all interested in the great truths of Christianity.

Maurice Becqué was born in Ghent, Belgium in 1912 and received his doctorate in theology from the University of Louvain. He is rector of the Redemptorist Fathers at Mons, Belgium, and is the author of many books.

Louis Becqué was also born in Ghent in 1914 and lives now in Tournai, Belgium. He is the author of eight books in religious fields and is a priest.

P. J. Hepburne-Scott translated *Life After Death* from the French.

THIS IS VOLUME

28

UNDER SECTION

II

THE BASIC TRUTHS

———

THE TWENTIETH CENTURY
ENCYCLOPEDIA OF CATHOLICISM

LIFE AFTER DEATH

IS VOLUME

28

OF THE

Twentieth Century Encyclopedia of Catholicism

UNDER SECTION

II

THE BASIC TRUTHS

IT IS ALSO THE

48TH

VOLUME IN ORDER OF PUBLICATION

Edited by HENRI DANIEL-ROPS of the Académie Française

LIFE AFTER DEATH

By *MAURICE BECQUÉ, C.SS.R.*
and
LOUIS BECQUÉ, C.SS.R.

Translated from the French by P. J. HEPBURNE-SCOTT

HAWTHORN BOOKS · PUBLISHERS · *New York*

First Edition, August, 1960

NIHIL OBSTAT

Andreas Moore, L.C.L.

   Censor Deputatus

IMPRIMATUR

E. Morrogh Bernard

   Vicarius Generalis

Westmonasterii, die XXXI MAII MCMLX

CONTENTS

INTRODUCTION

"Master, what must I do to achieve eternal life?" Happy man, we say, for he comes to question Christ, not about the existence of eternal life—he takes that for granted—but about the means to achieve it, the roads that lead to it. Happy man, for the fact of eternal life is something he holds as certain. Many of our civilized contemporaries, most of them baptized, have lost this happy certainty. Their question is not, "How can we achieve eternal life?" but the fundamental one, "Is there such a thing as eternal life? Honestly and truly, shall we rise again? Answer us, Master!"

"Master", I said. But it is no longer to him, to Christ, the one sent from the Father (sent, "that they may know thee"), that our post-Christians address their question. The prevailing fashion draws them elsewhere, or rather in four directions. The ignorant look for an answer in table-turning. Others, often practising Christians and comfortably off, strong in their semi-culture, are infatuated with oriental religions. There they seek for masters, for though they no longer believe in hell, they have an unquestioning faith in reincarnation. Abstruse works on Indian religions, heavily marked and annotated, occupy the place of honour on their shelves. But don't ask if they have ever read, marked or noted the Gospels, the Epistles of St Paul or St John! And while they are dazzled by these scattered lights to be found in all religions, they have turned their back on him who was the true Light, "who enlightens every soul".

"He was in the world, . . . and they who were his own gave him no welcome" (John 1. 9-10).

No welcome for him: and here we have the third category.

Those who refuse to welcome him—the last war has greatly swollen their number—so far from turning their backs on Christ, look him full in the face, but think he has nothing to say to them, for there is nothing at all, no heaven, no God: death puts an end to the tragic tale of life. We shall not rise again. Christ gives us no light, has nothing to offer us. The night of existence is unrelieved. Does this mean that from the bowels of the earth they have brought forth the light which their fathers drew from above? Has their refusal to welcome the future life flooded their hearts with joy and peace so as to make a paradise of this world, instead of the next?

"I am the Truth."

Light on the future life, the future life in God, man's future life, light on our resurrection, our two resurrections, either for life or death—like a rocket which, placed truly on its base, soars into flight, but, wrongly placed, fouls its start and plunges into the sea—it is Christ who gives that light, in its fullness, with authority. That is what this book proposes to show. Is it opportune at this moment? It is indeed opportune, for what our semi-Christians know about the resurrection, heaven, hell or purgatory, is so vague, inaccurate, diluted, caricatured, so mixed with childish or grotesque, distorted images, that it is only natural they should look elsewhere in their search for the genuine.

But this book is also addressed to our keen Christians, for the fourth category is found among them. Supporters of a Christianity which is social, committed, zealous for true charity, they have no use for a quest that is exclusively concerned with the salvation of the individual, for that would only be selfishness. The problem, in fact, is how best to combine one's own salvation with concern for the salvation of others.

This is only a short book. It will not require more than an evening or two to reopen the dossier of the "things no eye

has seen, no ear has heard . . . the welcome God has prepared
for those who love him" (2 Cor. 2.9). But perhaps you will not
think all this too stupid, too narrow, too naïve, too out of date,
too *bourgeois*, and that Christ has perhaps taught us some
positive and final truths, completely overwhelming and of
sovereign efficacy for life on earth.

The first chapter reflects something of modern literature,
so obsessed by this problem. The second reviews the attitude
on this question of certain modern currents in philosophy.
The third examines the idea of death and survival in other
religions, and the remaining chapters treat explicitly of
heaven, hell, purgatory and our resurrection. The book
concludes with the consideration of the purpose of life.

CHAPTER I

THE FUTURE LIFE IN CONTEMPORARY LITERATURE

"Since men have not succeeded in curing death," remarks Pascal ironically, "they have decided . . . not to think about it at all." It need not be added that they have never quite succeeded. Never has man been able to lead the untroubled life of the flowers or the insects, untouched, undisturbed by the idea of death, the future life, the "other world" and God, the wholly Other. They have come to the point of deciding—as we see in more than one contemporary—that this life, and matter, are all that exist, and that the question can be treated as dead and buried. But though buried, the problem of death pushes above ground again; it is the couch grass, always cropping up on the artificial lawns of our amusements, degradation and poses.

After century upon century of civilizations, after mountains of philosophical and literary works, after all the thinkers, all the wise men, all the poets, the problem remains. For Christians, for believers, the problem is solved: "I shall rise again." For the others, those without faith, death and the future life can only remain as an obsession, a question-mark and a kind of yearning.

Even if we do not put it to ourselves, the question forces itself upon us, whether we will or no. We are neither a pear hanging on a twig nor a caterpillar on the back of a leaf. About death, no one can say calmly, quietly, lucidly, that for him it is just a "biological phenomenon" which does not raise any problem of life, that it is without value, depth or dimension; that man, like the pear or the caterpillar, simply decomposes and life is finished.

How many novels there are, describing human anxiety! It is surely the very task and vocation of the novelist to analyse the heart of man. His heart and the hearts of his brothers, with or without the faith. Particularly does "dread" (*angoisse*) underlie our contemporary literature. The reader will readily think of scores of passages in his own language. Here are only a few examples which make one think, a few notes in the course of our reading, to which many others might be added.

Maeterlinck's plays are haunted by the mystery of the future life, a reality which cannot be grasped. *The Blue Bird* is but one of its names.

The children who pursue the lovely bird but can never catch it, discovered marvellous lands. The happiness they wanted escaped them, but their desire brought them joys they had not expected. In spite of all, they felt very happy. But it was only a dream! And the loving mother, to whom the little dreamers tell their adventures, offers them a humbler happiness which is born of tenderness: "You thought you were in paradise, but heaven is wherever we embrace one another!"

Maeterlinck clearly contrasts the dream with reality: reality is blessed by whoever loves it. But the author does not fail to recognize the homesickness of men, who feel they are exiled from their true native land, where perfect beauty is one with perfect goodness.

In *The Satin Slipper*, Claudel masterfully describes this unassuageable thirst of the human heart. The wound opened in the side of man to give birth to the woman signifies a lateral way (*latus*, side) to the contemplation and love of the infinite splendour. The wound of love can be cured only in heaven.

Prouhèze has good reason to say about Rodrigo, who loves her: "I alone can provide him with a need on all fours with his longing." She understands in the end what the angel had explained to her, that man and woman could not love "otherwhere than in paradise". The Jesuit Father, before he dies, thinks of his dear brother Rodrigo and prays for him: "Lord, it is not so easy to escape you, and, if he goes not to you by what he has of light, let him go to you by what he has of darkness . . . Make him a wounded man apart, for that once in his life he has seen the face of an angel . . ."[1]

Yes, a wounded man, for when God passes by, be his touch ever so light, it leaves a burn, an open wound, which it is beyond the power of human balms to heal. We are reminded of those famous words in the *Confessions* of St Augustine: "Thou hast made us for thyself, Lord, and our heart knows no rest, until it may repose in thee."

And there is that passage in which St Augustine regrets that he had come too late to love the eternal beauty: "Thou wert within me, and I without, and there made I search for thee . . . I pant after thee. I tasted thee . . . Thou didst but touch me, and I do even burn with a desire to enjoy thee. When I shall be perfectly united unto thee in every part of me, no labour nor grief shall be mine any longer, but my life shall be truly alive, being wholly filled with thee."[2]

Is not this what Henry de Montherlant avows when, time after time, he exploits the Christian vein in his plays? There is a love compared to which everything else is as nothing. It is the

[1] *The Satin Slipper*, trans. John O'Connor (London, 1931), pp. 130, 131.
[2] *Confessions*, X, 27, 28 (Sir Tobie Matthew's translation).

absolute which the king Ferrante in *La Reine Morte* calls to his aid: "O my God", he calls in his dying agony, "in this respite which is left me, before the sabre passes again and strikes me down, make it cut this appalling knot of contradictions within me, so that at least for one instant before ceasing to be, I may at last know what I am."[3] What I am? A man athirst for the torrents of the divine bliss.

To cut the knot? But that would be to cut the supreme privilege of man: to be *a knot joining the finite and the infinite*. When this knot is no more, man is no more.

How then can man escape God? Those who try to do so cannot help, in their novels, signalizing his "presence by absence".

Mauriac's heroes are well aware of it. In *Thérèse* and *The Knot of Vipers*, in *The Dark Angels*, *A Woman of the Pharisees*, *The Lamb* and *God and Mammon*, not forgetting *The Loved and the Unloved*, *The Little Misery* and *The Enemy*,[4] the same thirst consumes all these burning hearts. In the "desert of love", only the living water promised to the woman of Samaria can quench their thirst, for it springs up into eternal life: the heavenly spring which never runs dry.

Catholicism grips us by the throat! It tears Mauriac to pieces, and Gide too: "Always this war between what is reasonable and what is not." It would perhaps be risky to stretch this last saying so as to make it mean some sort of repentance or even regret. But François Mauriac was not wrong to bring it out so clearly. Perhaps Gide, the "immoralist", thought on his deathbed about what he once wrote to Du Bos about Pascal: "Oh yes, I know I cannot read again some of his phrases without being overtaken by a sob . . ." Gide adds that he did not like being thus gripped at the heart, but he

[3] *Queen after Death*, in *The Master of Santiago and other plays*, trans. Jonathan Griffin (London, 1951).

[4] English translations of Mauriac's works by Gerard Hopkins (Eyre and Spottiswoode, London, 1931—).

could not conceal his distress: "The man who says he is happy and who thinks, may truly be called strong." This is the confession of the man who wanted to experience all life and not to believe in sin. (*Les nourritures terrestres; La Symphonie Pastorale*).[5]

Sin? He returns to it in his *Journal*. It is an imprisonment from which Gide begs his Lord to deliver him. Pierre-Henri Simon remarks how fond this author was of quoting the words of our Lord in his profane writings. This is something more than just an "amusement". One must see it as a clear decision not to be really "impious". Thirst for fervour, the appeal to renunciation, aspiration to beatitude, all these sentiments shine out in the works of the man who claimed that no good literature could be made out of good sentiments.

Blasphemies, depravities, diabolical sarcasms by no means prevent this soul, so hungry for perfection, from sobbing in secret because it feels in itself the agonizing wound of the infinite. Always that wound.

Some think that this torment of Gide's is derived from his Protestant, even puritan upbringing, as well as from his special type of sexuality. But are these causes enough to explain the oscillations of this mind and heart? In *La Porte Etroite*[6] and *Nouvelles Nourritures*, the attentive reader will discover, beneath the repeated outspokenness, a mystical quest for a more than earthly happiness.

Younger authors, professedly atheists, betray the same longing. Is their rage for living just rash bravado? No; poor young Dean flung himself into the pursuit of life, full and boundless, but his wild career reveals not so much the restraints as the longing of his tormented heart.

May we not say much the same about Françoise Sagan?

[5]In *Fruits of the Earth* and *Two Symphonies*, trans. Dorothy Bussy (London, 1949).

[6]*Strait is the Gate*, trans. Dorothy Bussy (New York, 1956).

When a journalist asked her: "Why are the heroes of your plays all so tormented?" she replied: "Because they live with the thought of death." Her interviewer answered that there was always God. "Yes", she admitted, "God is a solution—but not mine."[7]

But when life—created by God—no longer has God for its solution, torment is corrupted into despair. Man's life is not, like a mathematical problem, capable of several solutions. It is either God or the creature.

There is a play, by Diégo Fabbri, *Le Procès à Jésus*, which re-examines our Lord's trial. Some Jews want to get at the truth about it and are going over the different charges recorded in the Gospels. In the course of the discussion a spectator interrupts to say: "The infallible sign of perfection, of the divine power, is victory. And your Christ always lost."

Whereupon "the blonde", his "girl friend", gets up and exclaims:

> He's a very intelligent man. Much too intelligent to believe, like you . . . Do you follow me? He's thought about these things all his life. Why, he was nearly converted! (*Laughs*) . . .
>
> Yes, he told me about it, one of those . . . nights. I had had one of those dreams . . . Oh, dear! how well I remember . . . Yes, he was tempted, he drew back at the last moment, and he turned against it . . . Now he has a grudge against you. You heard him?
>
> [The spectator answers:]
>
> "Excuse her . . . It is true . . . It is true that I got to the point of envying those like you, Sir, (*addressing the priest*) who have the faith. It is true that the faith must give you great peace. But I have the right to think that such a peace is too . . . easy. And many men nowadays are not prepared to buy this peace by renouncing their reason, they reject this support, this remedy for life, this hope of another, eternal life. Do you think this takes no courage? That it is not a torment?"[8]

[7] *Figaro Littéraire*, 1957.
[8] D. Fabbri, *Le Procès à Jésus*, French translation (Paris, 1958).

Always this torment of those who pursue their search against the stream of the human heart.

We find the same thing, in his own way, in another Italian author, whose *Le Métier de vivre* (The Art of Living) consists in defying heaven. "After all", he sneers, "blasphemy is a fine occupation for those who are not convinced of the existence of God, but feel him now and then under their skins. God will have his revenge . . . That's his system. He will put you in hell, but even if he turns the world upside down, no one can take away the grief he has experienced, the hammer-blows he has suffered!"[9]

How near to hate is love! These blasphemous lines are just one more proof of it.

Men cannot with impunity solve their problems by eliminating God. Distress leads them one day to the rejection of life, or to the unavoidable question: "Above ground, one is not lost. But afterwards? When one is under it?"

We have spoken of a wound: it is not only the scorching passage of God which causes it. To banish God from man, from the mind and soul of man—heart, mind and soul expressly made for God—is not to purify them from some foreign body, it is to resolve to leave them gasping for breath: you are opening on the finite an angle constructed to subtend the infinite. But since the finite, however you add to it and fill it up, can never equal the infinite, it is to leave heart, mind and soul unsatisfied. An everlasting wound . . .

[9]C. Pavese, *Le Métier de vivre*, Translated from Italian by M. Arnaud (Paris, 1958).

CHAPTER II

THE FUTURE LIFE IN CONTEMPORARY PHILOSOPHY

Let the reader make no mistake: we are not attempting here to describe all the views of modern philosophers on death and what follows it. This is only a brief sketch of two currents of thought characteristic of our time and of considerable influence on it. Philosophies have always been concerned with man's immortal destiny, with the undying element in him. But we can hardly deal with that here. It will be more to our purpose to describe in another chapter how peoples, rather than thinkers, have reacted to the fact of a mortal life, a life which comes to an end but longs to continue. This chapter aims simply at bringing out the views on human salvation of the Existentialists and the Marxists.

Neither Existentialism nor Marxism is a philosophical system in the strict sense. They are, we may say, intellectual movements, like-minded groups. Existentialists all have the same concrete manner of envisaging the mystery of existence. Marxists are concerned with the problem of happiness on earth, in a reformed society.

Both try to justify man's condition. They know that men

search for a solution to their anguish. So it is well to remember that the Christian himself is in anguish, even though he knows his destiny. "To be at ease is to be unsafe", as Newman loved to say. To be without anxiety is to be lost in advance.

We have first to clarify Christian psychology with regard to the observations of the Existentialists, after which the ideas of Marx and his followers will become clearer.

EXISTENTIALISM

The "anguish" (*angoisse*) revealed by contemporary literature, whether "committed" or not, has become an object of study for philosophy, since it, too, studies the impulsions of the soul. In fact the philosophies of our day have abandoned the serene regions of objectivity, essence and the universal for subjectivity, existence and the particular. Never before, perhaps, have philosophy and literature been so closely linked. These manifestations of modern thought deserve our attention because of their attitude to the future life.

In general, we can say that all these philosophies are more or less "existentialist". The upheaval of two great wars, the anxiety and insecurity arising from the overthrow of firmly established régimes and systems, have not been without influence on their development. Yet long before the shock of the first world war the Danish philosopher, Søren Kierkegaard, in *Fear and Trembling*, had analysed the tragic element of existence. The aesthetic attitude of abandonment to the present moment is untenable. Life is only made bearable by transcending the aesthetic and even the ethical sphere, to arrive by faith at the religious plane. This faith is truth, but "truth for me", and therefore pure subjectivity. Every truth is subjectivity. Man will be what he will be, according to the idea he forms of his being. His eternity is decided and planned in time. He will find God, who became incarnate to save him, by setting himself up as "I" before himself. The absurdity, the obscurity of the individual life, ineffable as is every individual thing, are experienced by the believer. But he commits himself only with fear and trembling, for he can never be sure of being chosen by the Lord.[1]

Subjectivity is sister to phenomenology. The famous professor Husserl (†1938), father of this new philosophy, seems to have been prepared to consider as "objects" only those to which consciousness applies. He confined his description to that which appears (the phenomenon) and remains identical, not concerning himself with essence or even existence. A thing is "put there" (ob-ject): it alone has a content which can be described to the subject, a content which consciousness applies. By limiting the perception of consciousness, Husserl gave a certain importance to the subjective and prepared the way for our modern existentialists.

Martin Heidegger continues Husserl's descriptive method but, in contrast to his master, applies it to existence itself. The only being on earth which is capable of conceiving that it exists is man. Human existence means being there, outside, along with things (ex-istere). It is, he says,"being-in-the-world", the Dasein. Death belongs to the structure of "being-in-the-world". It constitutes the last, supreme existential possibility. Because man is thrust into the world, he submits to its division. He reaches out to the past, the present and the future and is aware of historicity. Above all he looks to the future. By this aspiration towards what is to come he rises above himself. But what is to come is death, looming on the horizon: so far from passing through death to a fullness of being, he finds only nothingness before him.[2]

[1] Cf. R. Troisfontaines, S.J., *Existentialism and Christian Thought*, trans. Jarrett-Kerr (London, 1950), pp. 16-23.

[2] M. Heidegger, *Existence and Being*, trans. Douglas Scott and others (New York, 1949), especially pp. 67-78. (Also London, Vision Press.)

Less of a pessimist, more religious, nearer to Kierkegaard, comes Jaspers. His position is that every existing thing thinks of itself, feels itself and determines its being. It at once encounters obstacles, situations such as space, time, pain and guilt, which limit the tendency to transcendence. But Jaspers ascribes a high value to these obstacles. They prove that man can neither be self-sufficient nor find an end in himself, in his own existence. This existence reveals a relation with God, with his mysterious presence. By a free choice the human creature can attain to the eternal and absolute Being. The divine greatness, transcendence, is merged with what philosophers call immanence, that is, the fact of being within. Thus appears the "inwardness" of the living God, who is my own, to whom in the hour of anguish I can offer or refuse myself. In Jaspers' meaning, human existence, more vertical than with the gloomy Heidegger, has the power to rise from failure to failure, up to him who transcends all. Through this final step, its drama culminates, at the fall of the curtain, in the encounter with the unique Other.

The existential philosophies, then, are not unanimous in refusing the appeal from this present world to the divine "beyond".

In France, especially since the last war, a whole body of literature has sprung up in which the ideas called existentialist have been popularized. The leader of these thinkers in the line of Heidegger is Jean-Paul Sartre. More of a psychologist, perhaps, than a metaphysician, he has described with a master hand the *taedium vitae*, the incurable *ennui* in which human existence is plunged. Man is a being who is in process of becoming. He is nothing more, being "condemned to liberty". The "being-in-itself", unrelated to others or to itself, becomes consciousness in man. It questions itself and refers itself to the world. This is the "for-itself", a spark surrounded by the night. The "for-itself", or the presence to itself, produces "Nausea".

For "there is nothing left in heaven, no Right or Wrong, nor anyone to give me orders", exclaims Orestes in *The Flies*. And then, as Simone de Beauvoir puts it, "whether there is anyone in the depths of heaven is no concern of man"!

In his little book *Existentialism and Humanism* Sartre declares that his philosophy is "a doctrine which does render life possible". "There is no sense in life *a priori*. Life is nothing until it is lived." It is the man who gives a meaning to life, for it is he who exists. And "he exists only in so far as he realizes himself; he is therefore nothing else but the sum of his actions, nothing else but what his life is . . . Man makes himself . . . he makes himself by the choice of his morality." He defines himself, as far as he can be defined, by a "commitment". Sartre wants to help man. His existentialism is a humanism. It is "not atheist in the sense that it would exhaust itself in demonstrations of the non-existence of God. It declares, rather, that even if God existed that would make no difference . . . What man needs is to find himself again and to understand that nothing can save him from himself, not even a valid proof of the existence of God . . . It is only by self-deception, by confusing their own despair with ours that Christians can describe us as without hope." But he recognizes that "man is in anguish". This means that by committing himself he acknowledges his responsibility: he chooses not only his own being but all of humanity. Nonetheless, in contrast with classical humanism, man is not treated as his own end. "An existentialist will never take man as the end, since man is still to be determined." He does not shut himself up in himself, but remains "for ever present in a human universe". He projects himself beyond himself, and so causes himself to exist. His choice, which is inevitable and commits all mankind, is nothing to do with a free act, a caprice, as Gide would have it. Though it does not spring from any pre-established values, it will not be without merit. Man is sure of that. Does Sartre, then, provide a remedy, a solution for man's despair? He gives no proof of it. He is right, of course, when he says that the Christian, too, despairs of man. This is true in Pascal's sense, that man is all misery and weakness and must look to God for everything, for without him he can do nothing. What is man's life, asks the Bible, but sorrow and vanity? But Christianity transfigures this life from above. It believes that heaven has already visited the earth. For Sartre, on the other hand, there is no transfiguration, no justification, no beatitude. There is no salvation for man: he is "a useless passion".[3] There is no more hope; nothing is left but to live one's life, even though the really human life "begins on the far side of despair".[4]

Does Sartre believe that this far side exists? Although he is sometimes very near to Nietzsche, although he declares like Zarathushtra that the "death of God" liberates man, he nowhere states that the liberty recovered by the disappearance or rather elimination of the Supreme Being enables man to transcend himself.[5] Nietzsche, of course, exalted this transcending and, in spite of his almost satanic hatred of Christianity, necessary for the strong and the supermen, he offers his own Christ as a model. Not the "pale Galilean", necessary for the weak and the failures, still less the Saviour promising otherworldly rewards, but a strange character, constantly turned in

[3] *Being and Nothingness*, trans. H. Barnes (London), 1957, p. 615.

[4] *The Flies*, trans. H. Hamilton (London, 1946), Act III, scene 2.

[5] J. P. Sartre, *Existentialism and Humanism*, trans. Philip Mairet (London, 1948), pp. 24, 33, 34, 41, 50, 54-6. This lecture is perhaps the least read of Sartre's works, but it shows how he tries to "justify" man's existence. Here is a characteristic extract: "The existentialist . . . finds it extremely embarrassing that God does not exist, for there disappears with him all possibility of finding value in an intelligible heaven. There can no longer be any good *a priori*, since there is no infinite and perfect consciousness to think it. It is nowhere written that "the good" exists, that one must be honest or must not lie . . . Dostoievsky once wrote: 'If God did not exist, everything would be permitted'; and that, for existentialism, is the starting-point."

on himself, on his inner world, in which he finds intense happiness and profound peace. To those who will follow him Nietzsche promises access to the only true kingdom of heaven within themselves. That is their one hope. Sartre does not appear to share it. If in places he seems a Nietzschean, he is nearer to Marxism, since it is men's destiny of which he thinks.

With the Marxists, he sees "no salvation for man" except in "the liberation of the working class". But he will have none of the materialist's faith, because he does not agree to renounce the rights of free criticism, evidence or truth. Sartre notes that "millions of men find in it (materialism) a hope and the image of their condition", and concludes that it enshrines some truths, but that does not mean that it is "entirely true as a doctrine".[6] It is only a myth.

That, at least, was what the philosopher thought in 1946. It is possible that he has since developed, but all the same, he has scarcely convinced us that his existentialism is a humanism, this thinker for whom "hell is . . . other people!", who seems influenced by auto-eroticism, and concludes with the theory of nihilism.

Very different is Albert Camus, who has often been compared with him. He parted definitely and publicly with Sartre and they exchanged some sharp letters. Camus, moreover, cannot resign himself to the absurdness of life, and this is the ground of debate between him and Sartre. He sees only one question of importance for man: should he, or should he not, commit suicide? The logic of life implies suicide.

But actually he is the man in revolt. *L'Étranger* is the man who agrees to live, literally, as a stranger to himself, to his own destiny in the life beyond. He wagers for the present, against the future, against the Eternal, without hope. Sisyphus is content to toil up the cliff, his feet ever slipping on the scree. That is

[6]J. P. Sartre, "Matérialisme et revolution", in *Les Temps modernes*, 1946, pp. 1537-63; 1561-2.

his personal, present destiny, which has nothing to do with some "higher destiny . . . This universe henceforth without a master seems to him neither sterile nor futile . . . The struggle itself towards the heights is enough to fill a man's heart. One must imagine Sisyphus happy."[7] His happiness, precisely as a man, consists in doing something for one of his fellows, for the good of mankind. Thus the Algiers doctor, in *La Peste*, has no desire for holiness or a halo, the reward of the just in some other, higher world. The genuine *Justes* build their real, final city on earth. This cannot be the City of God and of grace. It is the city of revolt. By opting for this, man will be choosing solidarity, brotherhood, comradeship. "These are the true riches, for they are perishable", and Camus goes so far as to say: "The Christian society with its faith seems despairing."[8] Not that he does not admire Christianity. But he still thinks that the created world is his only country, the flesh his only certainty, and that "understanding" dies with it.[9]

In one of his Essays, called *Noces* (Marriage), he clarified his views about his world. This passage is worth quoting:

> I had spent my morning in a Franciscan monastery at Fiesole, full of the scent of the laurels. I had stopped a long time in a little court overflowing with red flowers, sunshine, black and yellow bees . . . Before going there I had visited the friars' cells and seen their little tables, each with a skull on it. And now the garden gave sign of their inspiration. I had gone back towards Florence,

[7]*The Myth of Sisyphus*, trans. Justin O'Brien (London, 1955), p. 99.

[8]"Remarque sur la Révolte," in *l'Existence* (in collaboration) (Paris, 1945).

[9]In *Les Justes* (Paris, 1950), it is interesting to read the legend of Dimitri, who had an appointment with God himself: "He was hurrying along when he met a peasant whose cart was stuck in the mud. So Serge Dimitri helped him. The mud was thick, the swamp was deep. It took them an hour to get it out and when they had finished Dimitri ran to the rendezvous. But God was no longer there " (pp. 123-4). The moral is clear: you must be either on God's side or on man's.

along the hill sloping down towards the town, open to view with all its cypresses. This splendour of the world, these women, these flowers, seemed to me the justification of those men. I wondered if they might also be the justification of all those men who realize that a certain extreme of poverty is always found along with the luxury and wealth of the world. Between the life of those Franciscans, shut away within their columns and their flowers, and that of those young folk on the Padovani beach at Algiers, who spend the whole year in the sun, I felt a mutual harmony. If they are stripped of everything, it is for the sake of a fuller life, not of another life. That, at least, is the only rightful use of the word *dénuement*. To be stripped always implies a sense of physical freedom and that accord between the hand and the flowers; that lover-like understanding between the earth and men sets one free from the human. If it were not already my religion, how gladly would I be converted to it! [And later:] The secret smile of Giotto's St. Francis justifies those who have the taste for happiness. [The Franciscans of Fiesole among their flowers had] Florence at their windows and death on their tables. A certain continuity in despair can give birth to joy.[10]

In passing we must note this concept of a "joy of the sun", which is the wealth of the poor. Camus returns to it in other essays, originally published when he was twenty-two, which he ended by republishing, without quite recapturing the style of those pages. In the preface to *l'Envers et l'Endroit*[11] he writes "Poverty has never been an evil to me: light flooded it with its riches. Even my rebellions were lit up with it. I think I can honestly say that they were always rebellions for all men, so that the life of all men might be lifted up to the light." After receiving the Nobel Prize for Literature the author, in his *Discours de Suède*, again returned to the ideas of his youth which he had never abandoned. Please God, this noble son of the Mediterranean, who believed in the splendour and "the beauty of the world", may have come to see before his death that

[10]*Noces: les Essais*, 39; 17th edition (Paris, 1950), pp. 83-4.
[11]*L'Envers et l'Endroit, les Essais*, new edition (Paris, 1957).

they are but the reverse side of a splendour and a beauty whose name is God.[12]

Earlier than Sartre and Camus, the philosopher and dramatist Gabriel Marcel had very soon come to know that life is both communion and mystery. Because it is communion, it establishes relations with the world. Because it is mystery, these relations do not derive from objectivity. They are not objects, presented to apprehension and understanding from without. Being is not reduced to having, and cannot become a problem. It is by meditation on his body that certain values are revealed to man. Thus in loving, another person is changed into a "thou" and a "presence" for the one who loves. The "I" finds a "thou". All the more does this prove true for the believer. In faith and recollection he discovers God, the "absolute Thou". He commits himself to the purely divine and is raised up to it. Now he can recognize God and bear witness to his ineffable, "transcendent" presence. But he must accept him and call upon him: his questioning must become invocation. If he is humble, he cannot refuse to pray. He will remain faithful and hold himself at the service of the things of God. He will foster the hope of being united to him, inasmuch as man, a traveller in this soulless world and bowed down under its technical sciences, is tempted to despair and suicide, and is in danger, too, of destroying the nobler values by regarding them as objects. But if he does, being is no more than having, presence is but matter, the person an image or a specimen, and God an idol. Man can only overcome these trials and conquer human anguish by coming to him "whose true name only religion knows": to God, his peace and his beatitude.[13]

[12] *Discours de Suède* (Paris, 1957).

[13] Cf. Troisfontaines, *op. cit.*, pp. 16-18. It is worth remark that there are some films which depict man's disquiet, such as Carné's *Les Tricheurs* and, even more, the films of Ingmar Bergman: *La Nuit d'un Clown, Le Septième Sceau,* and *La Prison.* These films point the anguish of the man who tries to pierce the mystery of death and love, of Good and Evil, and are a real metaphysical inquiry into the problem of the after life.

ANGUISH

Human anguish. Do you suppose that we Catholics, we believers, nurtured in the Light, have never to wrestle with it? I do not mean those "simple souls" for whose "faith of the charcoal-burner" there are no problems: after all, neither are other simple souls, who have no religion, troubled with metaphysical problems.

Perhaps it was to escape from such anguish as afflicted St Augustine before his conversion that Pascal, the believer, wrote an immortal masterpiece. And the saints? When St Paul admits: "If the hope we have learned to repose in Christ belongs to this world only, then we are unhappy beyond all other men" (1 Cor. 15. 19) he implies that he may well have experienced anguish. And when he says: "It is not the good my will prefers, but the evil my will disapproves, that I find myself doing", this internal cleavage is surely a pain which is sister to anguish. Yes, many of the saints have had to pass through deserts of the soul which we simply cannot imagine. Then nothing is left to them: neither the created world, for they left that behind at their starting place, nor God, for he has suddenly withdrawn himself. The saints have known anguish. All the more, therefore, many a priest, many a holy priest, many an apostolic winner of souls has at times felt the ground sink beneath a faith which is upheld only by the cord of an unshakable loyalty.

Anguish? But are we not men, like you, our brothers without the faith? Christians as we are, have we seen God, seen him with our eyes? We have not. And those who say they have seen him, are they so sure they are not subject to some illusion, some auto-suggestion? No. Has a single flame of hell ever appeared to us? Has the cry of a lost soul even once pierced our earthly night? Never.

We believe in God. We believe in an invisible heaven, an

invisible hell, because Christ has told us of them and because the Church, his ambassador, the only qualified interpreter of his word, faithfully transmits that word to us. Christ, and the Church by and in Christ, have given us their letters of credence —historical truth, the miracles, the life, the teaching. We know that they can neither deceive us nor be deceived. We have received the grace to believe them. But since we have not been able, like Thomas, to put our finger into Christ's wounds, nor plunge our hand into the fires of hell, nor pierce Paradise with our eyes, do you think that confronted with all these mysteries beyond reason, all this infinity unperceived by our senses, our hearts do not sometimes heave a sigh of anguish? Our senses and intellects are surely no less exacting than yours, and even if our soul does enjoy an untroubled peace, who can say that the winds of the world never ruffle the surface of our bodily nature? On the one hand, a certitude riveted to the soul; on the other, lack of evidence for the senses and the reason: is not the coexistence of these opposites in the same vital experience enough to produce, at intervals, a sensation of vertigo?

On the one hand we see so many atheists who seem to enjoy peace, so many good men who never pray to God, yet live noble lives. On the other hand we see the flagrant hypocrisy of so many Christians. Do you think this unnatural spectacle leaves us indifferent?

Besides, we live on two levels: the level of the divine and the infinite on which our souls live, and that of the human and the finite with which, like you, we are at grips. Our desires are fixed on heaven and God, but we have to dip our hands in the common dish of human life and at times to stand in the mire. This continual double displacement between our souls in heaven and our bodies on earth must sometimes bring us to the verge of tears.

Nothing is so sweet as true communion, nothing more

peaceful than a life lived in faith; but nothing is more delightful than those earthly joys, which the Christ of the Cana marriage-feast has not forbidden us to taste. To know that the good things of this world pass away—though their passing does not prevent their being good—and are no doubt all the more delightful and desirable because, as St Augustine felt, they are more fleeting; to love the good things of this world, to use them, to sit at the same table with our unbelieving brothers, but to have God in our hearts: can this continual mixture of the finite and the infinite, this duality of existence, be experienced without drama?

Duty and sacrifice rewarded so much too late; the wrath of God against the wicked never proved—for trials and disasters fall on the innocent as much as on the guilty, and earthly injustice bears often more heavily on the good than on the bad—can these mysteries leave us unmoved?

In a word, can you imagine that we can live out our state as men on this earth and never feel "nausea"?

But we know that in fact this is our lot in life. We are animals, and that is one fact. We are reason, conscience, spirit, and that is another. We are all that is earthly, and at the same time wholly an opening on the divine. The mixture of the two in the unity of the person (which is, as we said, a knot joining the finite and the infinite) cannot but cause anguish.

But that is man's privilege, that he is anguish.

Nothing can stop it being his heritage, his opportunity, his salvation. For whatever he may say, whatever he may make out, however hard he may try to prove the contrary, he knows that the joys of this world do not satisfy his longing. He knows that however he may lull his reason to sleep, drug it and "dope" it, he can never stop it dreaming of the infinite. He knows that however brilliant his earthly success may be, the human, the merely human, does not satisfy. Made of two natures, man needs the infinite as much as the finite, heaven as much as earth. Death cannot be death. "I shall arise". He feels it, he knows it. The ratiocinating reason may construct a thousand reasons for unbelief. A thousand and one irrepressible voices whisper: there is something else.

So why pretend? Why make ourselves out so strong, so clever? Says Simone de Beauvoir: "Whether there is anyone in the depths of heaven is no concern of man." But the water promised to the woman of Samaria, for which man still thirsts after drinking of all earthly springs—does that really not concern man?

And when you have exorcized God and shut out heaven, to become entangled and hobbled in your nauseas and your revolts, do you think that is cleverer? You cut out the infinite part of man, and the rest, being cut away from the infinite which gave it meaning, now disgusts you. Whose fault is that?

But, you say, that is what we like. This purely finite, which has no meaning, which revolts us, is the difficult solution. "The Faith must bring you great peace. I have the right to think that is rather too easy . . . Many men refuse this support. Do you think that takes no courage? That it is not an anguish?" (Fabbri, *Le Procès à Jésus*).

I answer: it is simply equivocation to proclaim that your solution is difficult; I agree that it is so, against nature, if you only take account of man's physical nature. This denial of our bent towards God is not a solution, not a good solution; well you know it. When you are trying to row against a stream which is carrying you towards infinity, it is not enough to say it is a difficult solution: you must admit that it is an aberration. Yes, I know that our brothers the rebels, the lovers of "nausea" ("Leave us alone to enjoy in peace the loyal bitterness of despair", says J. Rostand[14]) are not lacking in courage and a certain dignity on the level of this world. But to feed the minds of the young on glittering sophisms, to say: your life is finer,

[14]*Pensées d'un biologiste* (Paris, 1954), p. 112.

truer, more human because it lives on despair, because it stakes on the perishable, because it refuses all reward, because it does without God, because it toils up "the cliff, feet ever sliding on the scree", and so climbs without mounting—to trumpet abroad these sophisms is, by a monstrous inversion, to turn all this nausea, revolt, despair, nothingness, into gods, hollow gods to whom the rising generations, dazzled by their leaders, are going to sacrifice, for years to come, the best of their powers, their aspirations, their passion for life. What is the ideal offered to youth? To live wildly in the despair of life, to live a life already dead, worse than death.

At this point, anguish has become a god, a god of hell.

Man is anguish, but the believer resolves his anguish in his faith.

Can the literature and philosophies of our day, all born of despair, need further proof that *man cannot with impunity solve his problems by eliminating God*?

MARXISM

Karl Marx was a Jew. His thought and writings have a messianic flavour; his theories are reminiscent of the Bible.

The capitalist, or Marx's caricature of him, is much less "religious" than the Marxist. The latter is attached by nature to the concerns of God. The former accepts religion only as a sort of entertainment in the dull routine of his days and in order to possess an idea at the service of his will to power. The capitalist's religion, according to Marx, is an ornament and an ideology. But the capitalist is powerless to exploit this religion in the economic sphere. The disciple of Marx, however, while he hates religious sentiment, still retains the sense of God, in contrast with the man who worships Mammon, or "capital", in Marx's vocabulary. In vain does the Marxist deny divine revelation, the redemption of the world, the hope of salvation, the other-worldly nature of man's happiness, men's fellowship in God: unconsciously he accepts all these Christian mysteries, in his philosophy of life and the universe, his *Weltanschauung*.

First of all he retains his faith, an enthusiastic faith in science, the science of historical materialism. History is unfolded according to the materialist dialectic, for which all objective reality, even the mind, is matter. The discovery of this scientific socialism takes the place of all the holy books from Genesis to the Apocalypse. And it is the history of the class war, always repeating itself, down to the present day. Such are the postulates of the *Communist Manifesto*. Marx, in language that smacked of both the sociologist and the prophet, taught that this war had its ups and downs, according to the principles of Hegel's philosophy—thesis, antithesis, synthesis. But it would certainly culminate in the revolution of the proletariat and, when this was complete, in the coming of a classless society, perfect and pacific in all points. In the strictly historical field, these dogmas are far from accurate, though they claim to be historical and scientific. They appear as a new "gospel", to which the mass of the workers in Communist territory must adhere without question. In the meanest hovels the visitor may find the book of the new Messiah—in a handsome edition —taking the place of the Bible.

Anathema to the heretics who have corrupted the Master's teaching! They have been condemned to the stake of the new faith. Even Stalin and Tito have smelled of the faggot. Their judges called them "deviationists", journalists called them "lewd vipers". The most faithful interpreter of *Das Kapital* will always be the great Lenin! It is essential to believe the dogmas of the Marxist religion, of which the Party is the Church and Moscow the teaching authority.

Never say, then, that Communism is "materialist and atheistic"! These "godless" ones have an absolute, to which they devote a cult. They foster a *mystique* and adhere to values which they hold sacred. Further, they are stamped with the Jewish-Christian heritage of Karl Marx. The workers, or rather the proletariat as such, resembles the *'ebed-Yahweh*, the Servant of the Lord spoken of by Isaias. It alone hammers out the constant direction of history. By intensifying hatred and war between the classes it will hasten the great night, after which will rise the red dawn of the liberation of the human race. Thus was constructed an eschatology, a Communist doctrine of the "last things", which so influenced the early Socialists that in the nineteenth century they rejected, in several countries, social reforms which were in fact due to their influence. The German Social Democrats, for example, voted in Bismarck's time against the laws which aimed at better standards for the working class. Socialist reformers who accept these laws are Utopians and only retard the course of history, whereas capitalists who force the working class into ever greater misery are hastening it.

The convinced Marxist, therefore, will not hear a word of any alleviation of his lot. The class war would at once lose its bitterness. The proletarian must wait for the final salvation, that of "the last quarter of an hour". The enemies of the people will then be finally eliminated. That will mean the end of hatred, the death of egoism and the ending of oppression. The true Jerusalem will come down. There will be a "new earth"! And so, wherever Communism is established, men enjoy a foretaste of the final bliss. The struggles will end one day: classes will have been abolished throughout the world. Then will come the fullness of peace and happiness.

There is no need to point out the apocalyptic aspect of the Marxist hope. In parts it seems to be founded on a sort of secularized Christian hope. It throws into relief the truth, too often forgotten in the nineteenth century, of the solidarity of all creatures in the realm of salvation. Human beings bear together, for one another and through one another, the responsibility of their destiny.[15] It is not only individuals who are to be saved. All mankind is marching to its liberation: what is more, the whole of nature will share in man's happiness, for it will become malleable and permeable at will. Pure joy will abound in a better world in which it will be good to live, with no selfishness to foul the air. The original sin of private property will no longer produce the "alienation" of man. Such is the outline of the Marxist vision of the final, eschatological days: it depicts a sort of kingdom, the kingdom of unalterable love, complete peace, absolute security. It has the merit of reminding individualistic Catholics that the economic structure of the common life in society is of concern to religion. Its error lies in claiming to have a scientific character. In fact it results in a pseudo-religion, offering sacrifice to an absolute with feet of clay. The charity of Christ offered to men is founded on a rock: community—"communism"—in God. Only the "common denominator" of the grace of Christ makes all men brothers. This paradise of brotherhood, which it is our most bounden duty to bring about on earth, but which will only be perfected in eternity, is the true one, for while it is promised to the humble and the toilers, it is not only their own hope for themselves, but for all men, whatever their condition, for all have God for their Father.

The Jew Karl Marx does not fail to paint the Communist picture of the coming world in the words and images of the Bible. The prophet of the proletariat secularizes it, no doubt, but he cannot help exploiting it.

Some commentators have been content to draw a parallel between the kingdom of heaven and the future classless

[15]Marx says somewhere, with a certain irony and good feeling, how "easy it is for Hegel to treat the problem of captivity in a purely speculative manner, in his well-warmed study in Berlin, and to resolve all human contradiction on the plane of philosophical dialectic". "So long as there are women and children in the factories of Manchester working eighteen hours a day, I cannot consider myself free."

society, between the Church and the Party. Dr Marcel Reding, professor at the Free University of Berlin, has tried to show that there are genuine analogies between the Marxist doctrines and the themes of the Bible. To convince himself he has only had to analyse some of Marx's passages. The latter has certainly repeated and turned round the observations of the Psalmist, who asserts that the wicked man denies God because no man does right (Psalm 13). On reflection, he says to himself that in reality this Father in heaven does not intervene and does not exist. It is not God who procures our daily bread: it is money which dispenses it, and by so doing strikes down all man's divinities to make a market of them. At least that is what Marx affirms concerning, not the mystery of the Jews according to their religion, but the mystery of religion among the Jews as they are. The actual Jew in fact worships wealth.

As for actual Christianity, far from taking Christ's demands seriously, it has justified slavery, praised the condition of the serfs in the Middle Ages and approved the oppression of the proletarians. The social principles of the Christian religion place the righting of wrongs in heaven, thereby allowing them to be perpetuated on earth. Preaching humility and patience, they have excused the grossest injustices.

This is why Marx proclaims a sort of Messianism: he is convinced that man, by adoring a God in heaven, has undergone an "alienation". The values he has given to God he has stolen from men. The worship of God has lessened concern for man. Man must recover his true aspect, through liberty. This liberty consists in the faculty of accomplishing his being (*Wesen*), the possibility of changing his nature. Henceforth he must construct a new city, build the new man. This man will free himself from all that is foreign to his destiny. He will shake off all capitalist exploitation and will be able to get rid of all religious constraints. This liberation, according to the new Messiah, will constitute man's happiness.

It is true that the reign of liberty is founded on that of the present misery. It develops from the starting-point of that foundation. But none the less, it will one day assure the destiny of man, in this world. Man's last end does not, then, consist in some otherworldly happiness: Marxian Messianism places that happiness in this world, a world which in one sense will no longer be "earthly" or vile. That is the Marxian faith. Jean-Paul Sartre rightly says, "one goes into it as into a religious order". It involves accepting materialism, accepting (in Stalin's own words) that God does not exist, that the mind is a mere "reflection of matter". The militant worker "must believe in the directives of his chiefs". He admits the principle of authority. He believes in Marx and Lenin.[16] On this head Karl Marx, who thought he was giving the death-blow to religion as something created and imagined by man, founded a new one. For the "illusion" of the future life, the pipe-dreams of the "opium for the people", he substitutes the truth of the world below, the future Communist society, whose Messiah will be the proletariat, innocent of the sin of all sins, capitalist exploitation. This society, with no more exploitation, no conflicts, no classes, no property, even, will liberate and deify man. To the "alienation" of the human being will succeed the religion of work, which alone can bring in the earthly paradise.[17]

We are a long way from Christianity. But that is much nearer reality than Marx and his visions. It knows that perfect brotherhood on earth, the earthly paradise, is a Utopian idea. Man is and always will be a free agent, and therefore capable of evil and doing it. In the world's last days selfishness and quarrels will still be rife, in spite of all social and political

[16]J. P. Sartre, "Matérialisme et révolution," in *Les Temps modernes*, vol.1, 1946 (June), pp. 1537, 1555-60, 1563.

[17]C. Van Overbergh, *K. Marx, son œuvre: Bilan du Marxisme* (Brussels, 1948). It was in 1930 that the Marxist Institute of Russia published Marx's unpublished manifesto (1844) on religion.

systems. Unwearyingly to teach men charity, their kinship in God, is one thing. To predict that this will be realized on earth is another matter. The "red paradise" is promised for the "great night", but is the lot of the toiling masses changed into a life of delight by the hope of a heaven for other people?

Having rejected "the opium of the people", as religion seemed to him, has he been able to lighten men of their woes in this present world?

All the same, if it should be true that there is a heaven, a God, on the farther side: if it should be true that for all men, rich or poor, this life is a vale of tears: if, finally, it should be true that to bear one's cross for God and to work with all one's might for harmony in human relations earns us heaven and our union with God: then who lives in joy, light and peace, the Christian or the Marxist?

And who is more truly man?

CHAPTER III

WORLD RELIGIONS
AND THE FUTURE LIFE

PREHISTORIC AND PRIMITIVE MAN

It is obviously very difficult to find out much about the religion of primitive men. We are restricted to a few conjectures, based on what traces they have left behind.

The earth is perhaps four thousand million years old. Life does not appear on it for about two thousand million years. The earliest traces of the presence of man do not go back before the Quaternary period, which is only a million years. The evidence for this is the discovery of *Sinanthropus*, the remains of about thirty human beings some thirty miles from Peking. They resemble the *Pithecanthropus* of Java, whose cranial vault is very similar to the ape's. There are some other specimens of this earliest type of humanity. But there is no evidence as to its religion. Much later came the stage of "Neanderthal man". The fossilized men of this stage have the same anatomy and physiology as modern men.

Neanderthal man seems to have been only a *homo faber*, a practical man whose thoughts did not go beyond making his tools. He valued utility above beauty. But even if he was not an artist, he may well have been intelligent (*homo sapiens*), interested not only in eating and drinking but in prayer and worship. Is not prayer a kind of poetry, an art as well as a science? The human heart will always be a "machine for making gods",[1] as is proved by Neanderthal men. They were religious: they had beliefs and rites. Their numerous burial-places and their funeral ritual show that they believed in the unseen. They paid worship to the skulls of their dead, no doubt to preserve their memory. Excavations have proved that they had a regular rite of interment. We can only hazard a guess whether they were moved by respect or by fear. But it is legitimate to interpret the idea of death evinced by Neanderthal man as a desire to communicate with what goes on in the other world, when one's brother man has lost the breath of life. In some burial-places scientists have found offerings of food and, in the Drachenloch caves in Switzerland, many bones of bears, remains of a sacrificial offering.

After the Neanderthal period, belief in survival is certain. The Stone Age men believed in an existence beyond the grave. They fed their dead, tried to keep them in one position, bound them and mutilated them. They sprinkled them with red ochre, symbol of blood, and surrounded them with little images. They honoured and feared their dead, whose mysterious presence was something to be dreaded.

Animals do not bury their dead. Man is an anxious animal. He wants to keep in touch with the departed, to communicate with the other world and pray to the spirits.[2]

That the men of the Paleolithic Age preserved the skulls and bones of their dead was probably due to affection: that they sometimes broke the skulls may have been out of fear and reverence. In the Megalithic period, that of the monuments, they gave their dead a sepulchre, often in the form of the dolmen.

[1] F.-M. Bergounioux and J. Goetz, S.J. *Primitive [and Prehistoric] Religions*, in this series. These authors note that man is *faber* or *sapiens* according to his vital needs.

[2] Bergounioux, *op. cit.*

After these earliest men we must study those known as "primitive", because they lived or still live "on the fringes of the great civilizations".[3] Ethnographers have written much about these tribes, whom we call uncivilized and savages, though often they are not as barbarous at heart as many educated men. Moreover, as we well know, neither culture of soul nor purity of morals is always the heritage of civilized peoples.

Primitive man believes in God. To the majority of hunting peoples he is a very vague and distant deity: their faith is a sort of deism. To planters and agriculturists he is the god of the sky, but his presence does not always imply his influence. He is a lazy god.

The "totemism" found among primitive men marks the "mystical" bond connecting individuals with an animal species. There is nothing in this to indicate any aspiration to the sacred or the unseen. But animism, or spirit-worship, is more connected with the invisible and perhaps celestial realities. The spirit is a presence in absence, a power without a form. When the spiritual forces are those of nature, this cult is called Naturism; when it is connected with the dead, animism becomes "Manism".

The settled primitive buries his dead in a place which then becomes the border-line between the two worlds. The nomad abandons his corpses by the roadsides and leaves them to the hyenas, which thus become sacred animals. There are some who mutilate the dead out of fear, as prehistoric men did before them. The dead will be grateful and favourable if the living provide them with blood or a life-giving drink such as milk or wine. Their life is like that of men asleep. But if the rites have not been observed they will wander.

The ritual acts keep the dead quiet, transform them into the "defunct" and make them like the spirits of nature. It is

[3] J. Goetz, *op. cit.*

necessary to offer them provisions, arms and clothes, so that they will be satisfied and appeased. Animist tribes in West Africa, to control the spirits of the dead and their power, employ fetishes.

It may be of interest to say a word about some of these primitive peoples who still survive. The Kanakas of New Caledonia have no word in their language meaning "to die". For them, the "defunct" is literally "functionless" ("one does not die, one is *de-functioned*", say the southern tribes). The dead is an exile from visible society and the rites serve to aggregate him to the invisible sphere of human society.

In Polynesia, too, death is not considered an annihilation: it is the prolonged absence of the soul from its flesh, absence due to a hostile cause or to bad luck. The soul will wander about till it reaches its final home, near the sun.

The Polynesians are careful to practise a cult towards their dead by many ceremonies. It is the same with the Carajas. The Eskimos require their priests to put them in touch with the spirits.

While there are some primitives who doubt the existence of the other world, there are many more who firmly believe in it. Such are the Lancadon Indians on the borders of Mexico and Guatemala. They believe in another world, similar to this, but without sufferings or cares. They think of it as underground or, according to others, in the sky. The Aztecs of Central America hold that the departed live in an infernal abode under the earth, except for those, such as the warriors, who have been able to reach a celestial region.

Primitive men often think that death is contagious. Many make presents to their dead. They provide victuals for them in the tombs where they have buried them, often under a sort of mound.

From these few notes it can be seen that few indeed are the primitive men who do not have some relations with the other life. From the Kanakas of New Caledonia to the Pygmies of Africa, there is everywhere a sense of the things of the invisible world, which procure man's immortality.

THE ANCIENT EAST

The religion of Egypt

The chief characteristic of the religion of ancient Egypt is faith in survival. Man's spirit, the immaterial part of his being, continues to live on, in strict dependence on his mortal remains. The vault into which these remains are lowered becomes the abode of the souls. It is their shelter and resting-place; there they find bed and cover. But besides this subterranean life, to which the pyramids bear witness in stone, ancient Egypt early came to believe in less gloomy regions, outside the earth, where those who served the gods enjoyed their society and the joys of heaven. There was the kingdom of Osiris, the god immortalized by the rites of Anubis. Those over whom the same rites were performed would become the subjects of Osiris and live for ever in his domain, later known as the Field of Offerings or, among the Greeks, the Elysian Fields.

Then came the paradise of the sun. A statute of the dead was elaborated about 2,560 B.C., at the beginning of the Fifth Dynasty, under the royal family which came from Heliopolis. The right of entry to the solar paradise was given by ritual lustrations. At first only the kings could penetrate to the empyrean, but first their wives and then, by slow degrees, their families, their servants and their courtiers were admitted to accompany them, provided they had received the baptism of the dead. Many others then acquired admission to the company of the "Heliopolitans".

In order to obtain a place in the ship of the sun and reach its abode, or that of Osiris, it was still indispensable to fulfil certain conditions. A judgement was imposed, from which it was necessary to emerge successfully. The heart of the departed was weighed in a balance which tested its sincerity. But could the dead man really avoid exclusion from paradise by reading the Confessions in the Book of the Dead, in which he denied ever committing what were called "mortal" sins? Truly religious and honest men could not be satisfied with this recitation, this magic formula from a compilation for the service of the dead. Ancient Egypt had too lofty a morality to approve such pharisaism. On the contrary, it taught that men really had to answer for their deeds in the presence of God.[4]

Furthermore, to die means to go to one's *akh*, that is, to reach the face of the god. Egypt at first believed that only the kings were admitted to the possession of the *akh*, or supernatural power. But soon ordinary mortals obtained the same favour, represented by an ibis. Besides the *ka* or spiritual qualities, men have a *ba*, the symbol of which is the stork, consisting of the faculty of being nourished and transformed. It is through this animating principle that the dead man can move in the other world.

At an early date Osiris, born of Re the sun-god and Nut the goddess of the earth, became the chief of the dead and prince of the underworld. Although the king has jurisdiction in the other world and also governs the world of the dead, which is like a perfectly organized state, his authority has scarcely any effect. If order is to prevail in the city of the dead it must be based on a judgement at the end of the earthly life. A balance is placed before Osiris; Anubis, who formerly buried the heart, weighs it. The wicked fall under the sword of justice and are condemned to horrible tortures: the just will enjoy the life of bliss. There are some who escape punishment; at first, as we said, by using magic forms to plead their innocence, later by wearing a scarab, the figure of the resurrection.

[4]E. Drioton, "Egyptian Religion" in *Religions of the Ancient East* in this series.

In heaven the body is no longer indispensable, but in the underworld it shares the substance of the soul and perhaps ensures it. So from the sixth century onwards the Egyptians were careful to embalm their dead.

Survival, however, is not always enviable, even for those departed who are not subject to torture. They have to work. They are afraid of hunger, or having to eat their excrement, or being eaten by worms, which would be a second death. The devotion of the living towards the dead procures their happiness, especially through mummification and the funeral rites. No nation has ever shown such skill in embalming its dead, and Egyptian mummies, like their tombs, always excite the admiration of visitors.

From simple graves these tombs soon developed into monuments. There was first the *mastaba*, a deep vault surmounted by an oratory. Then were raised the pyramids, reserved for kings up to about 1600 B.C., then allowed for ordinary mortals. Finally there were many hypogea, tombs cut out of the rock. Above the vault was fitted up a chapel, just as a temple was built near the pyramids. Oratories, chapels and temples were used for the rite of offerings for the provisioning of the departed, a duty which devolved at first on the eldest sons and, later, on the priests of the cult. The inscriptions on funerary steles made appeals to the living, the dead imploring their help in the shape of bread, beer and other products.

The Egyptians had the merit of conceiving a heavenly life, the reward given to those who had deserved it. Some of them even realized that heaven gave the justified an intimate union with God, in the land of Osiris among the stars.

Religions of ancient Western Asia

The Hittites (3,000 B.C.) of Asia Minor and the Hurrites (2,000 B.C.) of Upper Syria used to cremate their sovereigns, the bones being anointed in oil and wrapped in cloth. They were addicted to magic and believed in myths, like that of the death of the dragon. But there is no proof that they believed in survival or immortality.

The Phoenicians, under Egyptian influence, not only built temples but also dug tombs—like those of Ràs Shamra—where the dead were given liquid offerings, evidence of a belief in a more or less material life in the other world. There the soul led a vegetative life, gloomy and monotonous. Its fate was tied to the fate of its bodily form on earth. It therefore needed offerings and rest, in a more hidden place, its eternal home.

The Sumerians of Mesopotamia buried their dead, either in houses, as the Phoenicians often did, or in cemeteries. They bestowed presents on them, to guarantee their subsistence in the life beyond. But the dead lived miserably in that beyond, where all was gloom and dust.

When the Babylonian dynasty was established in Mesopotamia, it was uncertain what the new religion would be. There was at first a pantheon, in which the gods of Sumer kept their precedence; Anu, the god of the sky; Enlil, god of the wind and the storm, who becomes "Bel" because he is the Father of the others. There is also Nergal, the god of the underworld or the "great land", the country of no return. There the dead slowly live out a life which is painful, miserable and even terrifying. It is dark, and for food there are only the scraps and rubbish left by the living, if these offer nothing better.

Such was the gloomy religion of the Mesopotamians.[5] Yet the Assyro-Babylonians seem to have believed in a different prospect for some men who, after a judgement, would be able to share in the life of the gods.

Iran and its prophet

The religion of Iran was greatly influenced by the doctrine of

[5] G. Contenau, "Ancient Religions of Western Asia" in *Religions of the Ancient East* in this series.

its prophet Zarathushtra, known to the Greeks as Zoroaster. He preached the eminent holiness of the "Wise Lord" or Ahura Mazda, whose kingdom was near at hand. After a revelation the prophet was inspired to predict the coming of a new world, where the powers of good would utterly and finally defeat the powers of evil. But in fact, long before the coming of their lord prophet, the Iranians had looked forward to the return of a golden age, but after a catastrophe. They also believed in a new life in the world beyond. The abode of the dead does not for ever appear as a fearful infernal abyss; it becomes a paradise. Its threshold can be crossed by those who are "clever and skilful enough to cross a bridge".[6] This at least was the primitive conviction of Iran, according to which, happiness after death was reserved for heroes and great men.

Zarathushtra retained the myth of the bridge, but made clear that it was the bridge of the Requiter (Bridge of the Chinvant). At the crossing of this colossal bridge (which is only an image, an accessory) the souls will be judged one by one. The sacred book, the Avesta, declared that this judgement of the soul after death decided its eternal destiny. Whoever can cross the bridge goes to paradise: whoever cannot, falls into hell. The Avesta teaches the resurrection of the dead and the transfiguration of the earth, but in a far distant future. On that day a gigantic cosmic cataclysm will shake the world. From one three-thousand-year period to another, after the coming of new saviours, the last judgement will be proclaimed and the universe will be renewed.

Zoroastrianism, also called Mazdaism, does not fail to punish the wicked. Their souls will suffer the worst pains ever endured by the living. When their conscience, under the name of "religion", appears to their horrified gaze, it will be personified by an immoral woman, hideous and foul-smelling,

[6] J. Duchesne-Guillemin, "Iranian Religion" in *Religions of the Ancient East*, p. 143, in this series.

in a state of decay, who will say: "I am your sinful actions . . ." And that will be hell.

But when the world comes to an end under a torrential rain of molten metals, hell and its inmates will disappear for ever. The space recovered by this disappearance will become earth, and this will be a paradise of perpetual delights.

THE RELIGION OF INDIA

The divine revelation vouchsafed to the Rishis or seers, the deposit of which is guarded by Hinduism, is contained in the four Vedas or Vedic books. The first, the Rigveda, is a kind of hymn-book. Among some thousand religious hymns is found the hymn for funerals, which calls on the dead to leave the living in peace.

Perhaps, then, the dead are to be feared. The Veda requires the formula of incantation to be read over them at the funeral service, so that their ghosts may not come to disturb the survivors. After the ceremony the dead descend to the abode of *Yama*, the god of the dead. They become immortal Fathers (*pitri*). But before they can gain immortality by a sort of dissolution of the soul in the universal soul, they must have broken the cycle of transmigrations or reincarnations and arrived at the "knowledge" of the absolute, the Brahman.

The central truth of Hinduism, moreover, is the concept of *karma*, which teaches that every thought, every action produces a good or evil effect which will have to be answered for one day, in this world or the next. This law involves reincarnation for every one who has not paid his debt. So these souls die and are reborn many times, till they have fulfilled their *dharma*, their personal duty. The purpose of all religion is to attain "Deliverance", when the individual soul is transformed into a particle of the Absolute. Systems of spiritual training called *yoga* lead men to Deliverance by progressive detachment.[7]

The Brahmin caste was responsible for expounding the Vedas or holy texts. But in the sixth century certain sects arose which, in the eyes of the official interpreters of the caste, were heretical. These were Jainism and Buddhism, which believe, roughly, that man must obtain liberation of spirit, but deny any need for rebirth or transmigration after death. Buddha rescues men from the river of transmigration. He helps them to land on the "other bank", whence no man ever returns. It is by asceticism, which has an educational value, that transmigration can be escaped, for it produces that indispensable lucidity which enables one to see how to avoid transmigration, and also to discern the true teaching.

Much later, Mandaism (*manda* = wisdom) and Manicheism insisted on this need of knowledge for eternal salvation. These are the two Gnostic religions (*gnosis* = knowledge). The former, which spread in Mesopotamia about the fifth century of our era, required the baptism of the dying; it provided anointings and prayers for them, to ensure their safe passage and ascent to Life, purified and pardoned. Manicheism came increasingly to see *gnosis* as the sole source of salvation, beyond the tomb. It is *agnosia* or ignorance which is the real evil: he who knows not is damned!

CHINA, TIBET AND JAPAN

The oldest of the Chinese religions certainly believed in survival and the existence of a heaven not very different from earth. The frontiers between the two worlds are ill-defined. In fact the day will come when heaven will wed the earth. The

[7]There are different Yogas: some exercises, e.g., of breathing, are both psychical and physical in type (the Hatha Yoga). Cf. S. Lemaître, *Hinduism*, in this series.

Chinese always honoured both, even before they gave thought to the relations between spirit and nature. Man's lower soul, which controls his vegetative functions, ceases to exist soon after death, in the tomb where it follows its body. The higher soul survives and attains happiness in proportion to its worldly knowledge and well-being. Like ancient Egypt, China has always practised the cult of the dead. To the sound of drums and bells they are invited to partake of the provisions and clothes represented by the votive tablets.

From the time of Confucius (born about 551 B.C.), the ancient religion lost much of its purity. This statesman, though universally venerated, was not a metaphysician; he was rather a somewhat positivist philosopher whose books enshrine the traditions.

Lao-Tse, rather earlier than Confucius, offers a better metaphysical and moral teaching, based on pantheism: "Life is the way of death: death is the way of life . . .while the *ki* (vital breath) coheres, the man lives; when it is scattered, he dies." In any case, life is only a dream, an appearance; nothing is of value, nothing lasts, nothing is either true or false! This explains the opportunism and the proverbial indifference of the Chinese mind.

When Buddhism entered China it underwent many changes and became less speculative. "In place of Nirvana it preached calm and tranquillity of spirit; in place of the total abolition of desire it preached non-action or, among the Confucians, respect for traditional rules and forms."[8]

The Chinese openly profess a kind of scepticism about heaven and hell. They say that these ideas on the future life were spread by certain bonzes or preachers under the influence of foreigners. No doubt, they say, there is some survival, but its duration depends on the importance of the deceased's social rank. As to the living, they have a duty to their dead and must

[8]G. Bardy, *Les Religions non-chrétiennes*, p. 240.

take care of their own health, for if a man is careless about this he offends his dead and causes them serious risks!

The Tibetans, too, fear their dead, whose influence may be either dangerous or kindly. They are afraid of being abandoned by their dead. By offering them libations every summer and preserving the ashes of their effigies the Tibetan "keeps a hold on them". Also, by means of a flag hung on a cord, stretched in front of his house, he communicates with them.

The Turko-Mongolian tribes of Central Asia believed in Shaman, the sorcerer. According to Shamanism, every man has five souls. The best, which is spirit, can be reincarnated. That of the wicked leads a wandering life which is dangerous to the living.

Japan has long practised a cult to the dead. Its national religion is Shintoism, which was modified when, about 552 B.C., Buddhism crossed its frontiers. But about a century before the introduction of Buddhism the Japanese gave up their too costly tombs. For some time longer they were content at most to maintain them with a numerous staff. In times of calamity they used to send them delegations.

The Japanese Nirvana is positive and combative in character. It enables a man to attain the dignity of Buddha by a series of victories over different worlds, those of hell, the passions and men. "The chief end of religion is always the enfranchisement of the soul."[9]

Throughout the Far East, in Indochina and the East Indian archipelago, faith in the life beyond is vigorous. The souls of the departed live in contact with the world of the living. The Indonesians think that they even live for a time among the living. The living give feasts to the dead, who so greatly need their offerings. The Minangkalams and the Khmers believe that the souls will be weighed and can make their flesh live again: others think they will be reincarnated.

[9]Bardy, *op. cit.*, p. 251.

GREECE, ROME AND BYZANTIUM

Ancient Greece disliked contact with the dead. Artistic and refined, they were afraid of being defiled by them. So the relatives of a dead man had to purify themselves after the funeral. Their religion hardly aspired to heaven for a better life. It turned rather to their Mother Earth, so fertile and nourishing. The Greeks worshipped it.

Like so many other peoples, they took for granted that there was a future life and that the living must honour their dead, so as to help them pass the gates of Hades, the dark regions under the earth. After the classical age, in the Hellenistic period, the masses came to embrace oriental or "barbarian" rites. A minority inclined to scepticism and atheism. Very few were ready to follow Plato and profess the immortality of the soul, but Plutarch († 127), on the threshold of Christianity, believed in it.[10]

The Etruscans, however, believed in a journey of the souls into the other world, as is proved by their paintings. Perhaps they believed that their dead survived after a fashion in the tombs. Their games and fights at the time of the obsequies were intended to obtain the favour and appeasement of the gods.

Coming from Asia Minor into Italy, the Etruscans exerted an influence on Rome. The origins of Roman religion, however, are still obscure, and its belief in a life in the other world seems often rather vague. Like the Indo-Europeans and nearly all peoples, the early Romans believed in survival. This is proved by their funeral rites and offerings to the dead. The dead inspired more fear than love. Those who died without being buried or provided for according to the ritual became miserable wanderers, always ready to torment the living. It was therefore

[10]Book XXIII of the Iliad shows that Homer believed in a life beyond the grave in which the souls, like shades, obtained through fire their rest beneath the earth.

necessary to reverence the dead like gods. Under the Republic they were called the *manes*, "the good people".

The cult of the dead continued to flourish throughout Rome's history, yet it seems that those who cremated their dead, in contrast to those who buried them, concluded that they were annihilated or banished far away. They continued, however, to make them presents. The religious system of Rome was greatly influenced by the East, and was a syncretism, a compound, a regular mixture of varied cults. Eastern gods were readily welcomed to its pantheon.

The "barbarian" nations, like the Germans and the Celts, looked for a better life after death. The former expected this sort of heavenly Jerusalem in Valhalla, at least for their warriors. The Druids of the Celtic religion (of Indo-European stock) taught a belief in the immortality of the soul. It was to this conviction that ancient authors attributed the heroic courage shown by the Gauls when their country was invaded by the Romans (*Pomponius*, Mela III, 29).

There seems little point in giving here a long exposition of the outlook of the Byzantine Church on eschatology. At the Council of Florence in 1439 the Easterns signed an agreement with the West. They accepted the beatific vision of the saints, immediately after their death. They granted that God's justice is applied to souls separated from their bodies before the end of time. Greeks, Armenians, Jacobites, Chaldeans and Maronites were thus reconciled with Rome. But on their return the delegates from Constantinople were mobbed and disowned: the monks had roused the rabble against them. In spite of these disputes the Orthodox Church, both Byzantine and Russian, adheres in practically all respects to the faith of the Catholic Church as to man's destiny in the future life.[11]

[11] J. Danzas, "L'Église Byzantine depuis le grand schisme," in *Histoire générale des religions*, vol. V, p. 339-70. The divergencies and special points of view of the Christian East will be noted in the course of this book. (Chapter VI.)

ISLAM

Mohammed, who was born at Mecca about 570, called his religion Islam, which means resignation and total abandonment to the will of God. Without necessarily leading to fatalism or passivity, Islam is characterized by submission to the good pleasure of God, to the decrees of Providence.

Mohammed's revelations were written down and preserved in a sacred book, the Koran, supplemented by the Sunna, or tradition. Despite its rigid monotheism the Moslem faith admits the existence of angels, the servants and messengers of God. Angels and demons are mortal. At the dawn of creation they were subjected to a test, and one of them failed in it: this was Iblis, the devil, who works with his evil spirits to injure man. They will have power to do harm till the general judgement. Until then the souls of the departed will lead a lethargic, torpid, unmindful existence, like men anaesthetized. They have appeared before their judge, however, at the time of their death and have been awarded their particular judgement.

But when the consummation of the ages dawns, they will be judged again and will be enabled to reanimate their bodies, which death had reduced to dust.[12] Those whose deeds weigh too light in the scales of the divine judge will have condemned themselves to the tortures of Gehenna. They will endure them for ever unless the Lord has pity on them. Their punishment is therefore not absolutely eternal. Some few disciples of the Prophet believe in everlasting damnation.

This is realistically described in the Koran:

> [The wicked shall be] in hot blasts and boiling water: and a shade of pitchy smoke, neither cool nor generous . . . ye shall eat of the Zaqqûm tree and fill your bellies with it, and drink thereon of boiling water, and drink as drinks the thirsty camel . . . We will

[12] Mohammed does not seem to have believed that the end of the world was imminent.

boil them with fire; whenever their skins are well done, then we will change them for other skins, that they may taste the torment.

This description is certainly calculated to terrify!

The other scale of the balance, which represents the delights of heaven, presents an equally highly coloured picture: rivers of delicious milk, exquisite wines, rivers of water of perfect purity will flow in abundance for the righteous. They will take their rest, in this paradise of pleasures, on golden couches, suffering neither heat nor cold:

> . . . on gold-weft couches, reclining on them face to face. Around them shall go eternal youths, with goblets and ewers and a cup of flowing wine; no headache shall they feel therefrom, nor shall their wits be dimmed! And fruits such as they deem the best; and flesh of fowl as they desire; and bright and large-eyed maids like hidden pearls, a reward for what they have done.

Mohammed never minimized the rather gross materialism of his views on the future life. But, though many modern Moslems do not reject this point of view, some great interpreters of the Prophet's thought have declared that beatitude is of the spiritual order and consists primarily in the vision of God.

The passages of the Koran which describe the joys of the life after death are undoubtedly of great beauty:

> Verily the pious shall be in gardens of pleasure, enjoying what their Lord has given them, for their Lord will save them from the torment of hell. "Eat and drink with good digestion, for that which ye have done!" Reclining on couches in rows; and we will wed them to large-eyed maids. And to them who believe and whose seed follows them in the faith, we will unite their seed with them: and we will not cheat them of their work at all: every man is pledged for what he earns . . . if he be of those brought nigh to God, then rest and fragrance and the garden of pleasure![13]

[13]*The Koran*, trans. E. H. Palmer, World's Classics (London, 1928), IV, LII, LVI. It should be noted that only the pre-Islamic religion of southern Arabia shows, by its hypogea and funerary steles, that it had a cult of the dead and a belief in survival.

The delights of this garden are not of this world. So, at least, declares the spiritual school which accepts the possibility of seeing God. The divine vision is the supreme reward of faithful Moslems, and of them alone. It will procure a joy "of excess", intermittent according to some, permanent according to others who have been influenced by the Christians and the Greeks.

All sin which has been repented is "effaced". There is therefore, properly speaking, no purgatory. Those who have shown no repentance will be punished. But if they have kept the faith, their punishment will not be eternal. The sinful believer, too, will one day be able to enjoy the torrent of celestial joys. Even if he does not repent his sins, he who believes will sooner or later obtain, through the intercession of Mohammed, pardon from the merciful Lord. Only he who obstinately refuses to believe in the one God and the mission of his Apostle commits an unforgivable sin and will undergo eternal damnation. For him, the ultimate mercy is of no avail.

There is, however, a super-terrestrial state between heaven and hell, a "neutral" place, a sort of "limbo", reserved for non-Moslem children and, temporarily, for adults whose good and bad deeds are of equal weight in the scales of divine justice. This place, called a'raf, has analogies with the purgatory of Catholic dogma. The dead live there in expectation and even experience a sort of purification, according to some authors. For merciful is the Most High, who has pity on men, his frail creatures, "formed of blood and slime".[14]

PROTESTANTS AND THE FUTURE LIFE

To draw up a synthesis of the teaching of the reformed Churches is not easy. They do not all follow the same articles of faith and their belief, far from forming a corpus of unchanging doctrine, varies from age to age and country to country.

[14]The Koran, VII, 124.

The tenet, however, which places Scripture above the Church, seems to have been adopted and accepted by all the Reformers. The Church is subject to Scripture, which is the sole authority in matters of faith. It is not the Church which expounds and interprets the word of God, but the word which explains and guides the Church.

Calvin pivots his exposition on the final resurrection, taking his stand on the holy Scriptures. He therefore considers eternal death from the angle of eternal life, and it is on the last day that men will arise, some to glory, the rest to hell. Then the supreme Judge will promulgate his definitive sentence. The Genevan reformer does not shrink from making clear how redoubtable is the "wrath of God", how fearful and un-natural to man it is to feel himself separated from the divine majesty.[15]

Orthodox Calvinists remain faithful to their master's teaching and even remind us that, besides separation from God, hell inflicts "bodily" sufferings. Their profession of faith therefore agrees in essentials with Catholic dogma as to the future life. But on one point there is notable divergence: Protestants deny the existence of purgatory. The reasons for this are easy to understand: they believe that Scripture says nothing about an intermediate state, in which souls are purified, between the vision of God and damnation. Moreover it is our Saviour's blood, his redemption, which cleanses sinners from every stain. To speak of a purification by fire, apart from the grace of Christ, is to derogate from the all-sufficing power of redemption. Finally, the absolutely free nature of salvation does not and cannot allow for any middle way between the accept-ance of some and the rejection of others. The elect show forth God's infinite mercy; the damned, his perfect justice. One and all, in their destiny, prove his unsearchable wisdom. Such is the

[15] *Institutes of the Christian Religion*, trans. Beveridge (London, 1957), vol. II, pp. 275-6.

teaching of orthodox Protestantism, which had a lively sense
of God, of his sovereignty.

In the eighteenth and nineteenth centuries the reformed
Churches had rather the sense of man. If one may put it so,
they saved man, rather than God. Their position seems more
optimistic than that of the "old guard" of the Reformation.
They are always keenly aware of the dangers of our earthly
state, but they take even more seriously the great mercy of our
Lord. They disassociate themselves from the earlier rigorism.
They lessen the gravity of serious sins. How can we understand
a grave mortal sin? How can we conceive a sin which entails
eternal damnation? The Protestants of the last century inclined
to think that once men were free of their corruptible, sinful
flesh they would repent of their frailties. The majority would be
saved. The really wicked would no doubt be annihilated.

Many Protestants then tended towards Origen's hypothesis
and believed in the "apocatastasis" or universal restoration of
all created things. They were far from the pessimism of their
fathers about predestination and had much less fear of hell.
But after the 1914-18 war the theology of the Reformed turned
back to the earlier traditions and positions.[16]

Two currents of thought are apparent: one goes back to the
teaching of Calvin, the other is inspired by the celebrated
theologian of Basle, Karl Barth. This great thinker rightly
insists on the primacy of Christ, the Word of God. He is the
Word incarnate, the divine utterance in person. To him the
Scriptures witness and on him they depend. They must be
interpreted according to him, with reference to his message.
Now Jesus proclaimed the love of his Father, his will to save all
men. God indeed condemns the sinner, because he is just; but
this justice operates "in Christ", as a witness to his love for us

[16]We need not delay to consider the "theology" of the many more or less
Protestant sects which are now trying to expand, especially in Latin
America (Adventists who believe in the imminent coming of Christ;
Jehovah's Witnesses who expect the speedy end of the world, and so on).

on the Cross. It is by a supreme act of love that God vindicates his justice. While we must not let excessive faith in man lead us to deny hell, neither must we minimize the power of Christ the Saviour, his invitation to feed on the grace of God, the immense pity of his heart. Love has vanquished hell.

Barth does not seem to share any of the horror which many of his co-religionists feel for Origenism. This is what he says:

In face of the danger represented by this conception, we must ask ourselves whether the peril of a theology which is sceptical and always critical, always doubting, because at bottom it is fundamentally legalistic and therefore terribly sinister on the essentials, is not in the end more dangerous than that of a frightening indifference or even of an antinomianism which could be effectively expressed by this doctrine. What is certain is that we have no right, in our theology, to dim the love which God has shown forth to men in Jesus Christ.[17]

Barth is obviously aiming a barbed arrow at those who have provoked a psychosis about hell. Is he wrong? All in all, he is careful to respect the revelation of Christ and not to treat it as a fable or a myth. Because he respects the Word of God, Barth sees in the Bible, which is God's witness, a rule of faith. Doubtless the Scripture, according to him, is only a word of man. It is not God speaking to us but the "place" in which he speaks to us and intervenes. Granted his transcendence, he cannot communicate himself, make himself known. But every believer knows him, and his Word, as it were indirectly, through a veil. Faith is response, self-abandonment, blind and utter trust. Though it cannot attain to the absolute Lordship of Christ, it saves man. The sovereignty of the Most High remains intact, but his redeeming Word justifies those who hope in it and cast themselves on its grace. This justification by faith, partly inspired by existentialism, resumes and really develops the

[17]J. Bosc, "Les Protestants croient-ils à l'enfer?" in *La Revue de Paris*, vol. 65, 1958, pp. 114-22.

first principles of Lutheranism. Barth reacts against the liberal ideas and doctrinal inconsistency of the nineteenth-century Protestants. He returns to the source of the Reformation. With the same intensity as Luther he feels the uncertainty of human life, the importance of salvation. And in so doing, far from raising a fresh barrier between the Catholic Church and his own, Barth brings them nearer together. What is more, his way of conceiving men's redemption, their predestination in God, seems in almost complete conformity with the dogmas of the Council of Trent, as they should be understood.[18]

While Barthians accept the doctrine of man redeemed, sanctified, received into Paradise through a faith which excludes neither hope nor charity nor obedience to the moral law, there has been a return towards rationalism on the part of certain German Protestants who favour the ideas of Bultmann. He has made it his task to reduce what he holds to be the opposition between Christianity and science. To this end he has tried to separate the Christian message from its covering of myth, to "demythologize" the New Testament. Influenced by Heidegger, he endeavours to interpret the revelation and life of Jesus in an existential sense. Man is nothing but dependence in relation to God, who gives himself to man in his Son. Man frees himself, appropriates the divine gift, the grace of salvation, by faith in the preaching of the Church. In the very act, his existence becomes "authentic". However, while Bultmann believes in the redemption of mankind by Christ and affirms that the death on the Cross is a historical fact, he rejects the truth of the resurrection which, in his opinion, is a myth. He makes numerous cuts in the sacred books and suppresses the life of the risen Christ and his ever-living presence in his Kingdom. A Protestant theologian was justified in remarking that Bultmann's

[18]H. Kung, *Rechtfertigung. Die Lehre K. Barth und eine katholische Besinnung. Mit einem geleitbrief von K. Barth* (Einsiedeln, 1957). In a prefatory letter Barth expresses his agreement with the author's exposition of justification by faith.

disciples were faced with the alternative of becoming Catholics or ceasing to believe anything.

Fortunately, many Christians separated from Rome feel that a return must be made to that Holy City which, as they admit, has remained faithful to the Gospel. They too desire to hear and confess the whole Word of God, to recover the message in its integrity. They will recognize the full truth of the divine mystery, hard as it may appear to them. They have therefore attempted to draw nearer to the Catholic and Roman Church.

Bishop Dibelius, for instance, President of the Council of the Lutheran Evangelical Church, paid a visit to Pius XII, and Pastor Asmussen described this as a historic event. He and other German pastors have formed a circle known as *Rassemblement* in which they strive to emphasize the truths accepted in common by all Christian Churches. Will this ecumenical movement lead to a general return to the fold of the one Shepherd at the approaching Council? And will our separated brethren profess their faith in the Church, one and holy, the sole plank of salvation in a sinking world, as Catholic doctrine understands it? How gladly would we all reply, with Newman, *Spero fore:* that is our hope!

CHAPTER IV

THE KINGDOM OF

HEAVEN

THE HOPE OF ISRAEL

Israel, a puny nation, in perpetual danger of extinction by its powerful neighbours, was the recipient of a divine favour absolutely unique in the history of the world: God chose it out and made a covenant with it. Yahweh spoke to it in many ways and by many means (Hebr. 1. 1). He guided it according to a time-table, an itinerary, a plan which he had settled from all eternity. He himself composed the story of "his" people according to his "days" and his ways. This story, like every other, looks towards an end and has no meaning apart from that end. That end, for Israel, was to be the final establishment of its kingdom. The messengers of the Lord, the patriarchs, prophets and kings; the fortunes and misfortunes of the Hebrews; Egypt, the desert and Canaan; the wars and the defeats, all lead up to the establishment of the "golden age", the new era. Prosperity and newness were to be the outstanding marks of the coming kingdom, for which the events of Israel's history were the preparation.

A new land was to arise, a new temple, a new heaven. A heavenly Jerusalem was to come down to earth. There milk and honey would flow, precious stones and metals abound; there the beasts were to be perfect servants of man. No sickness was to be seen there, nor old age, nor death, nor sorrow of any kind. Such is the backcloth of the great Hebrew hope.

But though expressed in terms suitable to Eastern feeling, this hope is very far from being a myth.[1]

These scriptural themes, which appear to be chiefly concerned with temporal favours, signify the abundance of spiritual values. The religious progress of the Jews is the condition and the measure of their freedom and happiness. They have a mission to perform. God will send them the king who will save the nation. According to the famous prophecy of Isaias:

Listen to me, you that are of David's race . . . Sign you ask none, but sign the Lord will give you. Maid shall be with child, and shall bear a son, that shall be called Emmanuel.

[And again:] For our sakes a child is born, to our race a son is given, whose shoulder shall bear the sceptre of princely power. What name shall be given him? Peerless among counsellors, the mighty God, Father of the world to come, the Prince of peace. Ever wider shall his dominion spread, endlessly at peace; he will sit on David's kingly throne, to give it lasting foundations of justice and right. (Isaias 7.14; 9.6–7.)

This expectation of a Messiah, a Liberator, was continually being developed by the Hebrews. They became conscious of their historic vocation and heritage. From the descendants of Abraham, to whom the promise was given, down to the predictions of the prophets, Isaias, Jeremias and the rest, the destiny of the chosen people is in one line and of one sort. It predicts and awaits the one who is to come and transform the whole world. "My spirit rests upon him", says Yahweh, "and he will proclaim right order among the Gentiles" (Isaias 42.1).

But he will himself be the victim of injustice: "here is one despised, left out of all human reckoning; bowed with misery, and no stranger to weakness, how should we recognize that

[1] A. Gélin, P.S.S., *The Religion of Israel*, in this series, p. 64.

face? How should we take any account of him, a man so despised?" (Isaias 53.3).

And if the Servant of Yahweh has been wounded for our sins, crushed down by our guilt (v.5), it is to bring us peace through his punishment. "God laid on his shoulders our guilt, the guilt of us all" (v.6). Servant, victim, yes, but equally King of glory: "I saw . . . how one came riding on the clouds of heaven, that was yet a son of man . . . With that, power was given him, and glory, and sovereignty; obey him all must, men of every race and tribe and tongue; such a reign as his lasts for ever, such power as his the ages cannot diminish" (Dan. 7.13-14).

The angel of the Annunciation was to repeat the famous prophecy of Daniel, to whom he had already predicted the coming of everlasting justice (9.24). Jesus often said that he was the Son of man, whose kingdom would have no end. Thus the Jews were able gradually to spiritualize their eschatological hope.[2] They came to believe that after death and "Sheol" they would have an eternal life through the resurrection, strictly so called. Was this already the belief of the prophet Isaias? In a beautiful prayer to Yahweh he seems to be expressing it: "Thy dead men shall live, my slain shall rise again. Awake and give praise, ye that dwell in the dust. For thy dew is the dew of the light" (Isaias 26.19, Douay version). Perhaps the prophet is thinking only of the rebirth and glory of the nation (5.14-15). Yet an anonymous commentator is sure that through Yahweh "death, too, shall be engulfed for ever" (Isaias 25.8). Israel hopes at least that the Lord God "will wipe away its tears" from every cheek (ibid.). "One lives on who will vindicate me," cries Job, "rising up from the dust when the last day

[2]Gélin, op. cit., p. 75. It must be remembered that the word "eternity" had no philosophical sense in the Jews' time, nor even in the New Testament. It meant a time without limit. The word used in the Scriptures, aeon, denotes either the present time (or present age), or that which preceded creation, limitless in the past; or else the time to follow the consummation of the world (the age to come).

comes . . . and in my flesh shall I have sight of God"
(Job 19.25-6).

The "little Job", as Psalm 72 is called, is equally sure of
final justice: "thine to welcome me into glory at last" (v.24).
Tribulation is valuable: riches are vanity. God will redeem
souls from the jaws of hell (Ps. 48.16).

The question of this "Sheol" will be considered later. The
Jews looked on it as the abode of the departed, who are only
shades, beings whose life is enfeebled, like a tenuous breath.
Death, which was brought into the world through the envy of
the devil, has destroyed the incorruptibility of human nature
(Wisdom 2.23-4).

Will death one day be overcome? This seems to have been
the faith of many of the Jews.

The invaluable discoveries of 1947 at the cliff of Ain Feshka
and of 1951 in the adjacent ruins of Khirbet Qumrân attracted
the attention of the whole world, and especially of biblical
circles. The famous Dead Sea cave, where a Beduin shepherd
found eleven jars containing rolls of parchment, was opened up
by a young Belgian captain, in spite of the obstruction of the
inhabitants. There in 1949 he brought Fr de Vaux, director of
the American School of Oriental Research. Exploration proved
that the famous rolls dated from the time of Christ, that certain
writings had even been composed before his time, and that here
was a Jewish library two thousand years old. Now, these
copies hidden away in the clay jars contained passages of the
Old Testament and other texts not received in the Canon of
Scripture. At Khirbet Qumrân, however, near the ruins of the
ancient fortress, the Dominicans perceived a large cemetery,
containing about a thousand skeletons. Archaeologists
deduced the existence of a religious community, and everything
seemed to confirm this hypothesis, especially as among the
"Dead Sea Scrolls" there was a document setting out rules of a

sort, called the *Manual of Discipline*. It laid down the obligations of the "monks" of the "New Covenant". Who were these monks ? Perhaps those Essenes, whose existence on the shores of the Dead Sea had been attested by several ancient authors, the elder Pliny, Philo and Josephus. This is not the place to examine the precise manner of life of this Qumrânite sect; we are concerned rather with its eschatological doctrine.

We must distinguish between the Writing of Damascus, already known to us from other sources, and those of the Qumrân sect in the strict sense, whose ideas do not always agree with it. The chosen people, suffering from hostile oppression, was anxiously awaiting its Liberator. The Damascus document promises that two Messiahs will come to save them. The second, called the Messiah of Aaron and Israel, does not play any particular part, as far as is known. But however that may be, Yahweh will come down to earth and, attended by his angels, will pronounce his judgement. He will make expiation for the sins of the just, who will be beatified together.

The ideas of the Qumrân sect differed from those of Damascus. They are contained in the *Manual of Discipline* and in a *Commentary on the prophet Habacuc*, the author of which, a "Teacher of Righteousness", tells the story of the war between the Sons of Light and the Children of Darkness. The monks of Qumrân profess a less collective eschatology than those of Damascus. They are contemplative souls, who meditate and strive to attain true moral perfection. Their holy quiet is not disturbed by the rise and fall of empires. The glory of a passing world cannot eclipse the hope of a little people. That is founded on the expectation of a "divine" being who will restore justice and power to the land of Israel. It hopes, too, to see the salvation of God. For Qumrân, it is true, this salvation has an individual character. Only the members of the sect will be able to contemplate God in the company of the angels. This contemplation is called "eternal life", because its

length is not determined, though it is not declared to be endless.
The Lord will purify their bodies in the hour of judgement.
They may then be able—it is not certain—to rise again. Some
hymns speak of a kind of resurrection. In any case it is certain
that the wicked, at least, will be punished. They will first be
subjected to the shame and scorn of the just, and will then be
burned in a gloomy fire.

Such, in brief, are the ideas of the sects of Damascus and
Qumrân on the coming of the times and the New Earth. In
spite of real analogies, it is very different from the Christian
dogmas on the last end and the life beyond. But these analogies
throw light on the statements of the New Testament in many
points. Both the form and the basis of the writings of the
apostolic community have been clarified in the light of the
apocryphal books of the famous monastery by the Dead Sea.[3]

THE TEACHING OF JESUS

The Qumrânite or Essene sect may have looked to a higher
life, even in a super-terrestrial sense, but the Hebrew people in
general envisaged only an improved earthly condition. Our
Lord had to strive to spiritualize the aspirations of Israel. On
this subject it is St Matthew who gives the clearest expression
to his teaching. He gives a fuller record of the Master's
parables about the kingdom of heaven than the other evangelists. It is he who constantly puts this expression on our Lord's
lips. He rarely uses that which is commoner with Luke and
Paul, "the kingdom of God". In all probability he sees a

[3] Abbé Michel thinks that the Qumrân sect did not develop in the
direction of Essenism, but was faithful to the religious and priestly ideal
of the Zadokites. While the Essenes hardly spare a thought to the coming
of the Lord, nor even to the presence of God and his angels in the sort of
empyrean where the souls go, the Qumrân sect, like that of Damascus
(Sons of Zadok), waits for the coming of the Messiah. It is, so to speak,
a para-Essenism, with an already individualist tendency on the subject of
salvation.

difference between the two expressions. To him, or rather to Christ, it is a land, a new earth, a world. There God exerts a special power: his reign and authority are extended over this world in a very special way. But St Matthew says more about the heavenly kingdom, which Christ has come to found, than of the reign or royalty of God. This kingdom, as is proved by all the Master's illustrations, will not be fully established till the consummation of the ages. On earth it is not and never will be more than a grain of mustard-seed. It is like a field in which the enemy has sown tares, where evil is mixed with good. But it belongs nonetheless to heaven, being a beginning of heaven, a heaven in the making.

The kingdom of heaven, here on earth, is identical with the Church, that is, the assembly of those who form the new Israel, the New Covenant. The concourse of the Hebrews at Mount Sinaï fore shadowed the community founded by Christ. Before it spread throughout the world this institution of Christ's comprised only a handful of men; the "Twelve", the apostles. Jesus instructed them. For them and for those who should follow them he promulgated the charter of his kingdom. It is found in the beatitudes, which form what we may call its fundamental law or constitution. Happiness is promised in this world to humble and pure hearts, to gentle and peaceable souls, to all who hunger and thirst after justice, or suffer abuse and persecution. Jesus bids them rejoice for their reward will be great in the kingdom of heaven. Living by this hope, they are already happy. The blessings we have now are not yet, of course, fullness; not the fullness of God. But looking forward to the perfect joy, our life is transfigured by it.

As Christians are no longer children of darkness, as they are ransomed by the Redeemer's blood, actually identified with the risen Christ, they are citizens of the kingdom of heaven. To speak more accurately, this kingdom belongs to them, but here on earth they have the bare ownership of it and only a partial enjoyment. The full usufruct will only be given them in the day of the Lord. They have been given an instalment of it. They possess the first-fruits of the Spirit, the Body of Christ, the Eucharist and the Church. The Church too is herself the Body of Christ. That is how St Paul expounds the teaching of his Master on the life of blessedness, which filled his heart to overflowing.[4]

As for St John, did he not say that the Word is Life and Light? Whoever hears the Word obtains his mystical presence, both in the future and now. Now; yes, this presence is here already, in virtue of the reality to come, of the Lord who is coming again. The beloved disciple is fully aware that he is mixing his perspectives: what is and what will be. St Paul had said that we shall be transferred into the Kingdom; St John says precisely that we have been enabled to pass from death to life, because we love our brethren. For him, as for his Master, it is by brotherly love that the love of God is perfected in his Son, that his return is made ready and that eternal life has begun (Rom. 8.11-17; 1 John 3.14).

This eternal life is divine because it is the peculiar property of God, who hands it on to his Son, and the Son of God in his turn communicates it to his own. It is a heavenly gift, and so it is grace: in other words, a free bounty on God's part. It is a supernatural endowment, offered to man, henceforth saved. In him the true life has begun. It follows that it is not merely an eschatological fact for the end of time. It is present, through Christ, through his bread and his Spirit. In sober truth, "heaven has visited the earth". This is exactly what St John thinks, even in his Apocalypse (12.10-11). As for St Paul, he makes it clear that there is no breach of continuity between the earthly and the heavenly life, for those on whom the Lord has bestowed a new and divine life.

[4]L. Cerfaux, *The Church in the Theology of St Paul*, and *Christ in the Theology of St Paul* (London, 1959).

We must never lose sight, then, of this truth, this reality that the coming world is not only a world "to come", for it already exists. And it is the Church of today which constitutes the "scene", as it were, of the heavenly, divine Kingdom. "At the last day, the Church will fill the world, Christ being wholly fulfilled in her, and God will be all in all."[5]

By this teaching St Paul accurately interpreted the thought of his Master when he said: the kingdom of God is within you (Luke 17.20-1).

THE THEOLOGY OF HEAVEN

The Bible promises beatitude to the just. Those who have found favour with God will be able to live eternally. This was already declared in the Old Testament, in the book of Wisdom (3.1-3; 6.21).

But in what does this eternal life consist? The New Testament has done away with the ancient dream of the Jews: the restoration of the kingdom of Israel in all its ancient splendour from the earthly point of view.

It was not easy for our Lord to rid them of this dream, even among his disciples. "Lord," they asked him, "dost thou mean to restore the dominion to Israel here and now?" (Acts 1.6).

Christ led them on and foretold the coming of his Spirit. The happiness he brings men is spiritual in essence. St John likes to use the words life, light and joy, but he does not make his thought precise. Will eternal life be fully experienced in light and joy, at the time of that manifestation of which he speaks, when we shall know at last that we are in the presence of God? Then "we shall be like him; we shall see him, then, as he is" (1 John 3.2). God's elect will "see his face" (Apoc. 22.4). But neither St John nor St Paul uses the precise language of the

[5] L. Bouyer, *La Bible et l'Évangile. Le sens de l'Écriture. Du Dieu qui parle au Dieu fait homme* (Paris, 1951), pp. 189, 195.

schools. Both think rather of the Parousia. The Lord will return and we shall be with him for ever (1 Thess. 4. 16, 17). And if this long-expected return should not be before his own death, Paul is sure that he will himself go to the Lord when he dies, without passing through Sheol.

Thus the first two Christian thinkers provide us with scarcely any details on the beatitude of heaven. They even appear to reject the possibility of contemplating God (1 John 4.12; 1 Tim. 6.16). But we know that this is corrected by other statements and there will be, in fact, a meeting "face to face".

It took centuries of Christian reflection to perceive its main outlines. Some of the Greek Fathers were reluctant to declare that beatitude implied the vision of God's essence. Theodoret of Cyrus († 457) said that it merely meant sharing his glory. In the middle of the fourteenth century John XXII held that the elect, before the general judgement, contemplated Christ's humanity, and only after that would come the beatific vision, but he retracted this doctrine at the point of death. His successor Benedict XII laid down that immediately after their death the souls of the elect behold God directly, without any intermediary. Is it possible to explain this vision? Scholastic theology attempted the task. Reason, it said, in order to comprehend heaven requires an intelligible form of this heaven to enter it (*sc.* reason). In the present case it is God who becomes this intelligible form (*species impressa*, the scholastics call it). He makes himself for reason, "representation", he effects whatever is necessary to let reason enter into possession of its object. He is still himself, God, that in which the intellect reads inside itself (*intus legere*) and says to itself that which is divine (*species expressa, verbum mentis*). Actuated by the intimate presence of the divinity in its very heart, the intellectual faculty receives from it a supernatural light, the light of glory (*lumen gloriae*), which radiates sanctifying grace in the blessed soul. Everything has been preparing it for the full reception of the beatific vision which it finally enjoys. Is it not in the nature of man to aspire to the "vision" of the infinite beauty? Certainly without faith this thirst for the divine would have been but a vague tendency, with no commensurate object, which could be only momentarily appeased by the possession of more or less ideal earthly beauties. Man's heart could not have defined its vague desire to the soul, nor say precisely what its dissatisfaction was. It would have been content to know the Creator of the world confusedly, somewhat "as in a mirror" (1 Cor. 13.12); to know the infinite indirectly, by refraction, by comparison, in the mirror of the finite. But God has indeed willed to unveil his face and to enlarge the human spirit so that at last it can see that for which, after all, it was created. For man it is the meeting, face to face, with God. We are overwhelmed. St Paul gives us this inexhaustible thought: he will be *all* in all (Col. 1. 17-20).

All! Beside the revelation of the Godhead in Three Persons, of whom the Second became incarnate; beside the divine perfections and decrees, the elect discover all the great mysteries of the faith. And so, therefore, the divine symphony and its harmonies: the angels, the saints, the multitude of the saved, the whole of creation. In the divine vision they rediscover the celestial bodies, the stars, the lovely earth—far lovelier than it ever appeared to their bodily eyes. They will see again their dear ones whom they left behind.

To speak more accurately, it is in the glory of the Word, splendour of the Father, that the blessed find again all they hold dear: all the blessings of this world. It is unthinkable that the God of love, in the abode of love, should turn all these blessings to naught. That alone which disturbs and distresses, that which does evil, will not touch their spirits. Yet through God's eyes they will understand the trials of those who are still on their journey through this world.

The joy of the elect will never end, for they can never sin again. The beatific vision confirms them in goodness. Seeing God as they do, says St Thomas, they cannot but love what he loves. They see too clearly to be deceived. Yet they do not all receive the same degree of beatitude. It varies in intensity according to each one's merit, according to the quality and capacity of love. Jesus said: there are many dwelling-places in my Father's house. Moreover, beatified souls obviously retain their personalities, their style, as we might say, their manner of being and loving, for heaven is not a beatitude in some Communist or Americanized fashion: plenitude in a dull, flat, undifferentiated state. St Teresa of Lisieux reminded us that glasses could all be full of a precious liquor, but of different sizes. Every person is unique. Everyone has received a unique call. The response is not some mass-produced welfare.

Theologians call those joys which accompany the divine vision and mount God's pearls, gathered in this life, in the crown of glory, by the name of "accidental beatitude". Martyrs and virgins, priests and doctors of the Church, will all have their special rewards. What is more, all the blessed will have their accidental beatitude increased, in the light of events which honour their Sovereign Lord and at the arrival of other souls in Paradise.

"Our being," writes Sertillanges, "in contact with God, does not renounce itself, does not lose touch with other creatures, and its beatitude must be enlarged, if not heightened, by whatever can come to it from its own natural functioning and its manifold relations."[6]

Then, too, the beatific vision does not produce a narrowing, as if it were a high degree of specialization, but rather an expansion of men's hearts. In the resurrection, beatitude will be truly complete, when our bodies too will be able to share in it.

[6]A. Sertillanges, *Catéchisme des incroyants*, vol. II, p. 235.

To say this is not to fall into a "carnal" conception of heavenly bliss; on the contrary, it is to appropriate an idea of the ancient Fathers of the Church, that the heavenly home will not know its perfect felicity until the end of the world and the resurrection of our bodies.

Hence we can see that if heaven is a "place", a region—and it would be temerarious to question it—it is still more an act and a state, a situation. It is the act of seeing God in his light, in unending ecstasy. It is also, therefore, a state: the abiding happiness enjoyed by the blessed. Heaven is therefore God and "ourselves in God", ourselves come from God and now returned to our home port.

There have been those who claimed that "pure love" of God requires us to renounce the joys of Paradise. This was apparently the opinion of Mme Guyon, who was directed by Fénelon and attacked by Bossuet. This heresy was condemned by the Holy See. It is of course absurd to close one's heart and soul against the joy of seeing God, under pretence of loving him better. In heaven, God is sought first for his own sake, because he is the Good; and then because he is our good. To dissociate love for God from the satisfaction of loving him, from the "wish for one's own beatitude" which lies in the beatific vision, is impossible. "God is the whole reason for loving, for he is the totality of good . . . Therefore the ultimate reason for love is that God is love."[7] In heaven, at least, we shall be simple. We shall love all, in the All.

[7] L. B. Geiger, O.P., *Le Problème de l'amour chez saint Thomas* (Paris, 1952), pp. 104, 120, 123.

CHAPTER V

DEATH IS ABOLISHED

If the gifts of reason and intelligence with which man is endowed lead inevitably to disgust with life, because it is doomed to end, why have we not been allowed to be merely animals or plants?

The rose, which lasts barely a morning, at least lives in peace. Ignorant of its approaching death, from the moment of its opening it peacefully enjoys its scent and beauty. The precarious condition of our life, as soon as we become conscious of it, introduces us at once to death.

"Why life, if death? Why death, if life?", says Dante. To think and ponder, turning over and over this dark problem, and then in the end to draw nothing from it but a philosophy of pleasure ("time is passing; let us enjoy ourselves"), or a philosophy of nothingness ("nothing rhymes only with nothing")—from such anguish, from such a load of living, the Christian is delivered.

Anyone who really tries to grasp our Lord's teaching on death will see clearly that for him it does not exist. The Master speaks of it to Martha: "I am the resurrection and life: he who believes in me, though he is dead, will live on, and whoever has life, and has faith in me, to all eternity cannot die" (John 11. 23-6).

Clearly our Lord means to teach Martha that, as Guardini so well brings out, something has happened to death. Man's last enemy is defeated.[1] We must never speak of it again! Henceforth it is resurrection that matters, life eternal and new, not death.

Following Christ's example, we shall speak of it only under this aspect. So too of the eucharistic promise, he says: "If anyone eats of this bread, he shall live for ever . . . The man who eats my flesh and drinks my blood enjoys eternal life and I will raise him up at the last day . . . Such is the bread which has come down from heaven; it is not as it was with your fathers, who ate the manna and died none the less; the man who eats this bread will live eternally" (John 6.52-9). Finally he declares: "If a man is true to my word, to all eternity he will never see death" (John 8.51). What does this mean? That for the disciple of Christ to die is no longer to die, it is truly "life". Henceforth death is like a sleep. Lazarus and the little daughter of Jairus "slept" because the Lord was going to raise them up, to waken them again to life (John 11.11-14; Matt. 9. 18-26).

THE GLORIOUS RESURRECTION

In the temple of Christianity the resurrection of our Lord stands out as the keystone. Christianity is undoubtedly Christ, embodying, revealing and offering the infinite love of God. But to succeed in this he has to save man, to destroy death, the "wages of sin" (Rom. 6. 23). He destroys it by his own death and resurrection. His resurrection prefigures, prepares for and procures our own.

Adam's sin had brought death into the world: "if death began its reign through one man, . . . more fruitful still is the grace, the gift of justification, which bids men enjoy a reign of life through one man, Jesus Christ . . . that so, where guilt held

[1] R. Guardini, *The Last Things*, trans. Forsyth and Brantham (New York, 1954; London, 1955).

its reign of death, justifying grace should reign instead, to bring us eternal life" (Rom. 5. 17-20).

This famous passage of St Paul shows that Christ's first objective was to tear up the decree of death and damnation which hung over mankind. To Adam in his disobedience Yahweh had said: "You shall die". Jesus comes to restore the promised immortality. In fact, he restores it in two stages: he procures us first an eternity of blissful life and then the glorious resurrection. No doubt there is a resurrection for the lost also, but it does not deserve the name, for it only confirms their damnation: "those whose actions have been good, rising to new life, and those whose doings have been evil, rising to meet their sentence" (John 5. 29). This is the real death. This saying of Jesus in St John's Gospel presumes that there are two kinds of resurrection, but St Paul reserves the name for that which is glory, life and light, by, with and in the risen Christ. He holds it to be the inestimable benefit of faith in Jesus. In common with all primitive Christian writers, Paul starts from the resurrection of the Lord and of Christians to prove the immortality of the soul. Because Christ is risen, the breath of life is not extinguished. The soul, which reanimates man's dust, lives for ever.

In the mind of primitive Christianity, the soul is immortal from the fact that the flesh lives again. And the resurrection of the flesh, of which Christ's is the promise, constitutes, along with the Parousia, the Christian's chief hope. Although in the order of time eternal life comes first, for it precedes the final resurrection, it is represented as only a consequence of Christ's victory over death. When that victory passes over completely into those bodies which are now "at rest", the work of redemption will at last be perfect. The paschal mystery will produce all its effects in the faithful on the day when they are raised up again. Baptism was the beginning of man's justification: the Day of the Lord will complete it. Man's physical death which consummates his sacramental death (prefigured by his burial in the waters of baptism), this death, with all the sufferings which are death's offspring, leads up to and culminates in the resurrection. The risen and glorified Christ becomes the new-built temple in which Christians live and step by step achieve their domination over death.

In the victorious Christ glorification has thrown down the barriers of time and space. Everything is present: his death and all the actions of his life. Distance no longer exists. The doors being shut, he enters the room where the disciples are talking together. He appears; he disappears.

So it will be for the elect. The breath of life will enjoy a higher power when next it animates their carnal bodies. In fact, their bodies will no longer be really "carnal": the soul will raise the flesh to its own level. Earthly conditions will be non-existent. Nutrition and procreation will be superseded by higher pleasures. In heaven they marry not, Jesus said, and the blessed will be as the angels. If the risen Christ was able to eat, it was because his glorification was not yet complete: it was so only at his ascension.

Cardinal Billot, that mighty scholastic thinker, has shown how the resurrection can be explained according to the principles of Thomist philosophy. He starts from the Aristotelian theory called "hylomorphism". The soul, in separation, keeps its characteristics. The body, on the contrary, in its state as a corpse, no longer retains anything of the individual which it was. All primary matter is pure indeterminacy, a potentiality of being. It owes to its "form" not only its existence but its properties, its determinations. When a man dies, his bodily remains become literally another being, under the effect of another substantial "form". At the resurrection its soul, its own soul, will communicate to the matter which it "informs" not only the breath of life but its identity.

This new matter, now "secondary" matter (that is, actually realized under another "form" or another principle of determination), this dust, if you like, will abandon its former identity through the power of a higher form, that of the spirit which takes it, "assumes" it. In this way the man's soul procures for any material particle its quantitative unity and all its other qualities. The chemical elements, molecules or globules, are of little importance: the resurrection restores to man his whole individuality. The soul, which contains it all, literally individualizes what it touches and reanimates. Such is the explanation of that prince of modern scholastics, Louis Billot. It exhumes, as it were, a hypothesis outlined by Durandus (1330), and buried for centuries. It seems to us very satisfactory.[2]

While the flesh recovers, or rather reclothes the personality of the soul, it is no longer at all in its earthly condition. The "glory" of this soul passes into it. The glorified spirit transforms it in its turn. The risen body, while preserving the integrity of its organs, is no longer subject to certain necessities. It no longer feels in the same way, it is spiritualized, "a spiritual body", as St Paul says. As has been remarked, this body will not suffer from defects or infirmities, nor exercise functions which in its earthly state were necessary for its support. The Apostle notes that the glorified bodies will be seen to be incorruptible: they will not be affected by pain, sickness or death, or moved by the passions. Untouched by physical or moral ills, those who rise in light will taste perfect love and the fullness of joy.

As Sertillanges so wisely says:

It remains to say that the body, raised up to respond to the appeal of the soul, can be reconstructed only in union with that soul which, as being the animator of the body, represents an internal art with its definite requirements, an architecture of forms,

[2]L. Billot, *De Novissimis*, p. 167.

an interplay of organs which cannot be separated without destroying the human identity.

Its sensibility will be not only preserved but increased; otherwise, says St. Thomas, the life of the elect would be no better than a sleep. Its noble pleasures will be like those of a banquet, though we need not draw on Mohammed for its details, and it is impossible for our mentality to picture its form.[3]

These delights will be ineffable, and no doubt varied and graduated to suit each unique soul, which receives and experiences them differently. Pleasure, freed from its heaviness, will at last be identical with joy. Bodies and souls will at last drink from the same springs. They will be no more two, but one in God.

THE LAST JUDGEMENT

Only at the end of the world will those who sleep in Christ share in his triumph and, in their turn, be victorious over death. All men, of course, will rise again. But, as we have said, only that resurrection deserves the name which gives the body its share in the glory and joy of the Lord, not in the pains of hell already endured by the soul.

This difference necessarily implies that there is separation at the last day. God, through his Son, will reunite his own. They will become contemporaries of Christ in his paschal mystery. That will be the Parousia, the glorious, solemn return of the Son of Man. The Easter victory will be consummated by the awakening of our bodies. The very world will itself be re-created.[4] Thus the consummation of the ages is the final act of our Saviour's redeeming work.

Parousia, judgement and resurrection should not be thought of as three distinct episodes of this act. They will be a single,

[3]A. D. Sertillanges, O.P., *Les fins humaines* (Montreal, 1946), pp. 123-6; *Catéchisme des incroyants*, vol. II, pp. 243 f.
[4]Rom. 8.21; Apoc. 21.1.

unique moment, bringing to a close the "passing", the Pasch of God among men.

The final redemption is our bodily resurrection (Rom. 8.10). The bodily resurrection and the last judgement are one and the same thing. And this judgement itself prolongs and consecrates that which is pronounced in the heart of every human creature.[5] Whence we see that in a sense the day of our death is already the end of the world for each one of us.

Yet more, the Parousia, the return of the Saviour-Judge, has already begun. At every moment, the Christian meets him on his way. In Holy Communion of course, but also when he welcomes children or the humble; finally in his last hour, the Lord silently comes in mystery. Doubtless this silent, mysterious return of Jesus (which will be considered later in connection with the particular judgement) does not reveal the brightness of his glory. Nonetheless, it anticipates every time the glorious coming of the Son of Man at the last day.

The minds of the early Christians dwelt most readily on the solemn Parousia of their Master; when the form of this world passed, then he would come: *Maranatha*, "Be it so, then; come, Lord Jesus" (Apoc. 22.20). This aspiration, so dear to the ancients, scarcely finds expression in the Act of Hope as formulated in our modern catechisms. This indeed has for its object heaven, and therefore the kingdom of heaven, or more precisely the eschatological reward, the "consolation", the joys of the reign of God. But it makes no allusion to the return of the Lord, judge of the living and the dead, nor does it refer to the resurrection. It is only in the Creed that we find these.

But for the liturgical and biblical movements, Catholics might forget to hope for the final Paschs! Now, while some respond vigorously, emphasizing all the wealth of our hope in

[5]John 5.21-4; 1 Cor. 3.13-15; 5.5; 1 Thess. 4.13-17; 5.9; Rom. 5.9-10; 2 Cor. 5.10; 2 Tim. 4.8; Phil. 3.11-14.

this expectation of Christ, the king of glory, and the decisive establishment of his kingdom, there are others who deny the second Coming, alleging that it was imagined by the early Church and inserted by her in the Scriptures. They would purify the New Testament from all its eschatological outlook. They want (in their horrible jargon) to "de-eschatologize" the teaching of Jesus. According to these Protestant theologians, Christ never spoke of a second Coming. His teaching and parables concerned the inauguration of his reign, in which men's hearts would be possessed and beatified by the boundless love of God.[6]

There is irony in the thought that the Modernists at the beginning of this century asserted exactly the opposite, saying that Christ thought only of a formally eschatological kingdom, the arrival of the world to come.

In reality, the Master's originality lay in revealing from the outset that this kingdom, which is truly the kingdom of heaven, comprises two phases. These subjects have been discussed, but we must recall them if we are to see the Parousia and the last judgement in their true setting. The first phase begins with Christ. With him, the Kingdom has "arrived". The Messiah has come, who drives out devils and forgives sins. He removes sorrows and raises the dead. He proclaims the good news to the poor, explains divine mysteries to the apostles and shows them his heavenly glory.[7]

But above all it is by his death and resurrection that the Messianic days are introduced and the New Covenant is founded. Now strikes the hour of Christ, and it inaugurates a new period for the kingdom of heaven. This period is still going on and will only cease when the second phase opens, on the Day of the Lord. This phase might then be considered

[6]C. H. Dodd, *The Parables of the Kingdom* (London, 1948); *Interpretation of the Fourth Gospel* (Cambridge, 1954); F. Glasson, *The Second Advent* (London, 1947).

[7]Matt. 12.27; Luke 10.20; 16.16; Mark 4.11; 9.1-12, etc.

the third period or era of the kingdom. It will proclaim anew, for the last time, the victory of the Lord.

"They will see the Son of Man coming, with great power and glory", prophesied the Master, quoting the prophet Daniel (Dan. 7. 13-14). He will send out his angels and gather his elect "from the four winds, from one end of heaven to the other". The evangelists do not state explicitly that this glorious appearance of the Son of Man will be accompanied by an act of judgement. But they imply it: the revelation of his glory involves the triumph of divine justice. The Lord has received the power to judge: he will exercise it on the last day. The parable of the tares teaches that "when the world is brought to an end, the Son of Man will give charge to his angels, and they will gather up all that gives offence in his kingdom, all those who do wickedly in it, and will cast them into the furnace of fire" (Matt. 13. 40-3).

St Matthew, who records this parable, elsewhere gives us a description of the last judgement. "When the Son of Man comes in his glory, and all the angels with him, he will sit down upon the throne of his glory, and all nations will be gathered in his presence". The King delivers a first sentence concerning those who are blessed by his Father: "Take possession of the kingdom which has been prepared for you since the foundation of the world." Against the others he decrees: "Go far from me, you that are accursed, into that eternal fire which has been prepared for the devil and his angels . . . And these shall pass on to eternal punishment, and the just to eternal life" (Matt. 25. 31-46).

The just are those who did not fail to help their brethren and love them; the others are those who had no charity, those who trafficked in iniquity, who have been ashamed of the Son of Man.[8]

So there will be accounts to render at the Lord's return,

[8]Matt. 7.21-3; Luke 13.28-9; Mark 8.36-8.

"talents" to exhibit (Matt. 25. 14). The elect, the good, those who repented, will be for ever with Christ in "paradise".[9]

The last judgement is universal, literally "catholic", in character. It is pronounced on the whole mass of mankind, on all men, "the living and the dead". It will be delivered on all nations, in some way assembled and forming one family. No doubt our Lord declares that the twelve apostles shall sit "upon twelve thrones, and shall be judges over the twelve tribes of Israel", under his presiding power (Matt. 19.20). These twelve tribes symbolize the new Israel, and therefore Christians. Does that mean that only Christians will have to appear before the tribunal of the Son of Man? The Church has understood that the entire human race will have to stand at the bar. The seats of the Twelve, then, refer rather to the Apostolic See, and to a judgement which means government, that is, to religious authority in the earthly part of the kingdom.

The Church knows that in her all mankind can escape death and share in the divine marriage-feast. The Son of God, said the Fathers, has wedded mankind, by his incarnation. Whoever breaks the marriage bond with the divine Spouse breaks it also with his people. In this way the general judgement shows the social side, the community aspect, of the redemption. God has willed to save his own people. Those who refuse to be associated with God's people will be devoured by the fire. Those who in any way belong to the new Israel will be purified by another fire: the fire of love will present them to Christ, as his Bride, with "no stain, no wrinkle, no such disfigurement; . . . holy, . . . spotless", on the model of his Mother, the Virgin Mary (Eph. 5. 27).

The whole earth will be present at the heavenly marriage, foreshadowed at Cana. Did not this earth, with the sky and

[9]Luke 23. 40-3. St Paul and St John also speak of the garden of delights or "paradise", to denote the heaven of the blessed (2 Cor. 12.4).

the sun, bear witness to Christ, in the hour of his passing? It too will therefore be judged and transfigured. Old things will have passed away, and all things will be made new.

When this present world is brought to an end, created things will again bear witness to the King of glory. However, these "signs in heaven" and the plagues on earth must not be considered one-sidedly or under too dark colours. It will rather be the enemies of Christ who will be withered up with fear and shudder with horror. It is not so much for Christians as for them that the end of the world will prove a catastrophe. For the former, Jesus bids them compare his coming to a blossoming, as in summer. It will be his apotheosis.

They are wrong, then, who want the world to come to an end speedily, by a cataclysm. Their desire is morbid: it thinly veils a foundation of selfishness, especially in those who are embittered by age. They cannot endure that the world should survive them, for others to enjoy. Their private world is about to end, so everything must end at the same time. Such are their apocalyptic predictions. But no man knows the hour. And may we not suppose that the Christian era, or our present nuclear civilization, is only in its beginnings? See what St John says in the Apocalypse:

> I saw a new heaven and a new earth . . . I saw that holy city which is the new Jerusalem, being sent down by God from heaven, all clothed in readiness, like a bride who has adorned herself to meet her husband . . . Here is God's tabernacle pitched among men . . . He will wipe away every tear from their eyes, and there will be no more death, or mourning, or cries of distress, no more sorrow: these old things have passed away. (Apoc. 21.1–4.)

THE PARTICULAR JUDGEMENT

Jesus said to the penitent thief: "This day thou shalt be with me in paradise". "This day" is obviously to be taken in an analogical sense. It means that the penitent sinner, who asked our Lord to remember him when he came in his kingdom, was entitled to enter the kingdom of heaven as soon as that was possible: when the executioners had done their work, or, perhaps, after our Lord's Ascension, without much purgatory, in virtue of Christ's promise and also of his own expiation on the cross.

One thing is certain: not only is man's fate decided at the end of time, it is fixed at the hour of his death. "The world is judged already", said the Master, and he meant to signify that he is himself the judgement of the world.[10] But if the world which hates him, the unbelieving world, has been judged and condemned, a particular hour strikes for each human being to appear before God: the hour of his death. While the last judgement underlines the collective aspect of redemption, the particular judgement emphasizes its personal character.

Whatever we may think of a type of theological socialists, more enamoured of the salvation of the world as such than concerned about their own salvation, it is nevertheless true that every one has to respond to the personal call of our Lord, to the demands of his love. This response of course implies brotherly love in the first place. That is obvious. But every man will have to give personal account of it to his God. In the very moment of his death he will see that the end has come. He will examine and judge for himself, in his soul and conscience, in his judge's presence and enlightened by him, the deeds and aims of his life. No one who calls himself a Catholic can have any doubt as to this particular judgement.

Furthermore, the Church has stated that death constitutes both an end and a beginning: an end, as being the term set to the testing-time of earthly life; a beginning, by giving access to the other life—or to the other death, the only death which really deserves the name.

[10]John 3. 18; 5. 24. The unbeliever is already judged.

No man's death is profane, since it is the ransom-price of sin, of original disobedience in the first place (Gen. 2. 17). The death of the second Adam has conquered the last enemy of the human race. One who dies in a state of grace leaves behind the time of probation. He is fixed: his heart and his love rest for ever in God. His gaze is withdrawn from the transient: he is now, in Mallarmé's words, *tel qu'en lui-même enfin l'éternité le change:* "as in himself at last eternity changes him".

His bodily death, remember, is the consummation of his sacramental death, wrought by his burial in the waters of baptism, which fits him into the pattern of Christ in his death. This death issues in resurrection (Rom. 6. 4-9).

The pilgrim has reached the end of his journey. A new life opens before him, the life he has chosen. It is the climax of his earthly life. His destiny is settled. *Alea jacta est* (The die is cast). The Epistle to the Hebrews links this ending with the redemption accomplished once for all (Hebr. 9. 28).

As soon as the soul leaves its body, it hears God's sentence. Its reward is at once decided. Perhaps, after some necessary expiation in purgatory, it will be the beatific vision. We have explained that the earthly phase of the kingdom of heaven is divided into two stages, that which precedes and that which follows the resurrection of Christ. Similarly the heavenly phase is like a diptych. Death instantaneously inaugurates man's eternal condition. Before the plenitude of bliss which follows the bodily resurrection, there will be, there is already, the beatitude of the soul which, though not perfect, is no less real and is superior to all the joys of earthly life.

The particular judgement is therefore marked by two qualities: it is irrevocable and it is immediate. A decisive sentence, an immediate execution of sentence: heaven, purgatory or hell.

Why is human destiny thus fixed at the moment when the soul leaves the body? More than one theologian says it arises from the very fact of separation. A soul in a state of separation no longer thinks or feels in a fragmentary, unstable fashion, at the bidding of its bodily condition. The flesh, changeable and frail, no longer interferes in the choice made by the pure spirit. Its choices as to the supreme end of its life will be decisive. The immutability of its fate springs from its final will, rather than from God. "The soul", wrote Billot, "remains immobilized in the disposition in which the stroke of death overtakes it."[11] This attempt at explanation does not eliminate the mystery of how the temporal is inserted in the eternal. How can human frailty, operating in the present, produce an absolute fixity in eternity?

Certainly, at the moment when souls leave the world and the flesh, they are illuminated by God, whom they see in his Son, their Judge. In him, at his judgement-seat, they become aware of what they are, what they have done and are worth, of their merits and demerits. But why has the die been cast? Why can they not make their last throw in the other world, to rectify their earthly performance?

It was the opinion of St Bonaventure, Vasquez and Ripalda that the blessed, and even the souls in purgatory, were still in a position to merit, if not their essential reward—the vision of God—at least certain lesser, "secondary" blessings. They scarcely won approval, any more than did Origen and his followers in the early days of the Church, who expected a final, general conversion (ἀποκατάστασις τῶν παντῶν).

In every age, it is true, attempts have been made to mitigate the doctrine which arrests man's fate inexorably at the hour of death. But how can they be reconciled with the mind of the Church? Does she not state that death puts a term to man's journey and reveals its final result? Did not our Lord make plain that both the rich man, who had no pity for Lazarus, and the foolish virgins, arrived too late?

[11]Billot, "La Providence de Dieu" in *Études*, 1923, p. 397.

Still, "theologians commonly admit that a special grace of conversion is granted to the sinner in the hour of death".[12]

Canon Glorieux tried, some time ago, to show that the last act is made when the soul parts from the body. It is then that it decides, full in the light, with increased lucidity, for the good. He wanted to avoid making death seem like an ambush or the assault of a cut-throat. When, on leaving the body, the scales fall away from the eyes of the spirit, the soul sees more clearly; though laden with sins, it can better appreciate what is at stake; enlightened by God, it takes sides once and for all, for or against him, with full knowledge and consent. This last chance would allow of the lost being restored *in extremis*. But in spite of himself the canon makes the soul's final choice fall on the other side, on the eternal slope, at a point when the separation is already a *fait accompli*. It would be better to place it at the actual moment when it happens; otherwise we could not be sure that death burns all boats and removes us from the changing to the unchanging.[13] In any case it is essential to remember that while death makes our wills irrevocable the composition of that will is conditioned by our whole past. It is not just one isolated act, apart from its context in life, but the whole activity of our life, with all its weakness and strength. The merits or demerits of the metal thus forged determine the final choice in the light of Christ. Our last moments are the falling fruit, which is good or bad according to what the tree's sap, good or bad, has made of it. Fr Troisfontaines rightly

---

[12]A. Michel, *Les Fins dernières* (Paris, 1927), p.32.

[13]Glorieux, "Endurcissement final et grâces divines," in *Nouv. Rev. Théol.*, 1932, pp. 865-92; pp. 882 f. De Brandt slightly corrects the canon's thesis. He develops and deepens it by commenting on a statement of St Thomas, that the angel merits, not at a distance, far from the end of his journey, but placed at the end of the road (*Angelus meret ut viator, non quasi distans a termino sed ut in termino vere existens*, Quodl., IX, art. 8; *Christelijke eschatologie*, p.47).

says that "each one will be for all eternity exactly what he wills to be".[14]

Does this mean that there are no deathbed conversions? But the divine judge, up to the end, is the Good Shepherd who pursues his sheep with unwearied tenderness. Doubtless special graces are given us in that hour. From his lips into our ears (like the priest in the confessional, like the doctor who tries a last injection) Christ can pour into us his grace of light. We must believe what St John says: "If our consciences condemn us, it is because God is above conscience, and nothing is hidden from him" (1 John 3. 20).

DEATH, RESURRECTION AND PAROUSIA

Franklin is right when he says: "In dying, we achieve birth". All life labours painfully to be delivered of this Life beyond death. For if, as Claude Bernard says, life is death, we must at once add that death is life, at least for those whose death is not abortion. "All is now beginning!" said a holy priest before he expired, and many others have uttered words of serene hope in their last hour. Charles Maurras, deaf from infancy, said to his chaplain, "At last I hear someone coming!" Even when a Christian's death is accompanied by dread and anguish, it will always give light and peace in the depths of the soul. In the *Dialogue des Carmélites* the prioress apparently dies in terror. Bernanos himself showed that in his last moments he had to cross swords with his ancient enemy. "Come on, then!" he cried, when agony seized on his tortured body.

Be that as it may, the words of the dying Oscar Wilde have often been verified: "The Catholic Church is the only good Church to die in!"

[14]R. Troisfontaines, S. J., "Hypothèse philosophique sur la nature de la mort," in *La Revue Nouvelle*, vol. 29, 1959, pp. 360-76; pp. 365-6. The author adopts Glorieux's thesis on the soul's final choice at the moment of death.

Here we must add that the act of dying is not in the nature of an "escape" out of the world. It is an act by which man forms and chooses new relationships with the invisible and even the visible world. The final choice, made in a more vivid and lucid consciousness, enables a better union to be established, in the light of God, with the world of men.

Again let us repeat that the Christian's salvation cannot be thought of as a selfish enterprise, an "every man for himself", an *après moi le déluge*. Our young militants are rightly scornful of bourgeois caution, of a life-insurance attitude, of the sanctimonious unconcern which can be covered by the words: "I have only one soul to save."

They are right in thinking that our last end is not only to save our own souls but to save the world, even the temporal world: "I was hungry and you gave me food." Who can blame them for not wanting an "individualist" spirituality? After all, the divine Master came down to earth primarily to found the kingdom of heaven, which was to be the new Israel, the chosen people, reconstituted as the Church, which has become fully Catholic in heaven.

All the same, we must never forget—and the danger is not unreal—the *personal* aspect of salvation. In *The Son of Man*, Mauriac notes this remark by a Marxist: "The marvellous thing about Marxism is that I have no concern for my own salvation." Yet in every city, the citizen's first duty is to order his own life aright in the city. Every Christian has to form a living stone of that building which is the Church; the first stone he has to shape is therefore himself. Christ tells us that God calls every one of us by name, as the shepherd calls his sheep. Each one owes it to himself to give a personal response to this call. To be saved, to behave rightly, to be deified, is our primary task, but this salvation, this behaviour, this sanctification, so far from isolating me from that of my fellow man, can only be accomplished by saving, sanctifying, building up the life of the community.[15]

"I shall rise again": that thought should be present to one all one's life, so that the whole of life may be a preparation for its most important act, that in which it culminates.

"The dogma of the resurrection", writes the modernist Turmel, "is the keystone of Christian eschatology. After Christology, the resurrection is undoubtedly the dogma which holds the first place in the ecclesiastical literature of the first centuries."[16]

That is perfectly true, and that is why the early Christians so earnestly looked forward to the moment when they would see Jesus again. Their *Maranatha*, "Come, Lord Jesus!" became a prayer which was spontaneously repeated during their liturgical meetings.

For some years past theologians have increasingly dwelt on the thought that with our Lord eternity is inserted into time. After his resurrection, history unfolds on another plane. The eternal operates in the temporal: the future has lost its indeterminacy. In other words, what was yesterday is not inexorably finished, rolled up, eliminated; what will be tomorrow is no longer that which does not yet exist, pure becoming, a future reality without consistency, like a nebula. The glory of Christ has released things from their temporal

[15]"This only goes to show that, even in the so-called "ecclesial" sphere we are very soon confronted with the danger of a collective docility and an anti-individualist diffidence about the individual, which we, sworn foes of individualism as we are, had not in the least expected and which ought to alarm us. Are there not already, here and there, among those who believe and are outwardly obedient to the Church, phenomena of disaggregation in the field of personal religiosity, of moral self-education, of asceticism, etc.? Is it not necessary, then, even within the Church, to defend the individual, his rights and still more his duties, in face of what is merely ecclesial?" Karl Rahner, *Dangers dans le catholicismed'aujourd'hui* (Paris, 1958).

[16]Turmel, *Histoire de la théologie positive* (Paris, 1914), pp. 179-80.

prison. And whoever belongs to Christ through the sacraments, the theological virtues, grace and the Mass, keeps what was, and already obtains what will be. It is only sin which will leave no trace in him and will be decisively past, effaced; partially in this life and totally after that purification hereafter which is called purgatory.

By our Saviour's victory over death, all things have been made new and heaven, the new Jerusalem, comes down to earth. So much so, that Christians should not imagine that their destiny is only to ascend beyond the stars. We must adopt a new outlook: the end of created things is that God comes down, pitches his tabernacle among men and grants them the joy of his intimate presence. This process has begun and is going on. At the last day, when, by a sort of remoulding, the risen men and women have come to their full stature, the descent of the heavens will change the face of the universe.

That is why it would be wrong to postpone the settling of accounts to the end of time, without reference to the present. We must never forget what Jesus said; that the world is already judged, since he has come and is always coming, he who is the Judge of the world. It is necessary to recall this point with some emphasis, before we close this chapter on death.

Fr Daniélou, quoting Fr Mollat, states this forcefully and clearly:

> Between the inauguration of judgement at the time of Christ's coming, and its fulfilment at his coming again, Christian life in its entirety is thus a continual judgement. The mystical presence of the Son of Man in all men imports an unsuspected eschatological dimension into all human relationships, that is to say, into all history at all time. Man is now face to face with the Son of Man at every moment of existence: the judgement is now . . . The resurrection of Christ is presented as the first and decisive

act of the last day . . . everything essential has been secured already.[17]

That is the Christian vision of the history of God and men, and its climax is the victory of Jesus Christ over death.

[17] J. Daniélou, S.J.: *The Lord of History*, trans. Nigel Abercrombie (London, 1959), p. 272.

CHAPTER VI

THE SUFFERINGS OF
THE FUTURE LIFE

HELL

It is a plain fact that many Catholics no longer trouble about hell. Do they still believe in it? A certain writer thus discusses the question:

> This rejection of hell is indeed a remarkable development, more important than the capture of Constantinople or the discovery of America. Why has no one ever written, besides the history of battles and treaties, the inner history of man? When once man ceased to admit, as a self-evident truth, that his deeds in this life entail dire consequences in the next, he was no longer the same. Henceforth, a sin or a crime, provided they remained hidden or did not become amenable to justice, no longer moved him to remorse or atonement. Unbelief guaranteed his impunity. This was a spiritual revolution more momentous than the intellectual revolution we owe to Galileo and Copernicus.[1]

The preachers must bear their share of responsibility for this revolution. There is a fashion for a certain type of sermon, which likes to seem sympathetic to modern sensibility and observes a bashful silence about the dogma of eternal damnation.

[1] Quoted by H. Rondet, S.J., *Un seul corps. Un seul esprit. La communion des saints* (Paris, 1952); p. 104.

Claudel, that man of robust faith, was shocked by this concession to the times. He recalled that Jaurès was haunted by the idea of hell; an idea, he wrote, of which "half the Gospel is full". A slight exaggeration, perhaps, but he was thereby reminding us that the word of God is a sword, that the herald of Christ has no business to be playing on pipes to conciliate sinners, leaving the salt of the Gospel to lose its savour. The existence of hell is a dogma, a truth revealed by God and proposed by the Church to our belief.

How is this revelation set forth in the Bible?

The Old Testament

It was only gradually that the Hebrews came to speak of sufferings to be endured in the other world. They believed in the survival of the soul; that breath of life which the Creator had communicated to a creature of flesh. Out of this flesh, basically only dust, the divine breath makes a living soul, in his image. But when the breath of life leaves the body, it does not die but dwells in "Sheol". There it leads a diminished sort of life, mute, lethargic and silent. Sheol is represented as a sort of underground abode, an abyss. The Latin Vulgate translates the Hebrew expression by the word *infernus* or *inferus*: "that which is beneath".[2] While the bodily remains become again what they were, a handful of dust, the soul goes down to the depths of the earth, a subterranean land whence none returns, where "there will be no doing, no scheming, no wisdom or skill left" (Eccles. 9. 10). There it is dark; not a ray of light penetrates. This aspect of darkness has been described by Job, even more vividly than by the psalmist.

"A land of darkness, death's shadow over all", where gloom and disorder prevail and the very light is like black night (Job 10. 20-2). Yet poor Job is so crushed by his trials that he

[2]The Greek rendering of Sheol is Hades (ᾅδης), literally, an invisible place.

longs to disappear into this dark chasm! "Waiting for what? The grave is my destined home: among the shadows I must make my bed at last: . . . mother's and sister's greeting the worms shall offer me" (Job 17. 13-13).

Does the groaning wretch despair of a reward after death? Is his suffering endless? Will the light be quenched for ever? Job is convinced of the contrary: "This at least I know, that one lives on who will vindicate me, rising up from the dust when the last day comes. Once more my skin shall clothe me, and in my flesh I shall have sight of God" (Job 19. 25-6). So his reward will come, for the Lord is just.

The Jews had tried in vain to maintain that happiness and hardship were distributed on earth according to each man's merits: they knew that this was not enough. Gradually they were forced to admit a sanction beyond the grave. The divine Requiter owes it to himself to be fair. The chosen people came to understand this better and better. Yahweh cannot be content with rewarding or punishing the nation. Israel comes to see that a distinction must be made in the other life between the good and the wicked. Sheol cannot be the permanent abode of those who fear their God. They will emerge from it: "Thou wilt not leave my soul in the place of death, or allow thy faithful servant to see corruption" (Ps. 15. 10-11), says the innocent man to his Lord, whose face he trusts to contemplate one day, when he awakes (Ps. 16. 15).

"My life God will rescue from the power of that lower darkness." But those who have turned their backs on him will lie there, huddled together like sheep. This shall be their portion for ever (Ps. 48. 15-16). Taking his stand on the justice of God, the psalmist contrasts the sinners' lot with that of the just.

The great prophets of Israel, too, insisted strongly on the judgement of God. Sheol reserves its direst sanctions for those who have offended Yahweh. A day will even come when the friends of God will rise again to eternal happiness. It is no longer question of the restoration of a Jewish kingdom, but of the wakening of the wise in the life to come. "Many shall wake, that now lie sleeping in the dust of earth, some to enjoy life everlasting, some to be confronted for ever with their disgrace" (Dan. 12. 1-2). This statement in the book attributed to Daniel is made clearer in that of Machabees: man can keep "hope in God, that shall raise up the dead" (2 Mach. 7. 14). And this hope in the resurrection to life, which only the good will share, encourages prayer for the dead: "these had made a godly end; could he doubt, a rich recompense awaited them?" (12. 43-5). The fire and the worms will not devour them for ever. "I, death's mortal enemy, I, corruption's undoing" (Osee 13. 14).[3]

Thus the Hebrews came to realize that sooner or later justice would be done, and that not merely on the national level but in the sphere of the individual, of the good and the bad. This is evident in the Scriptures, which speak more than once of a final and definite reckoning. The wicked will be punished. True, Israel does not place this punishment with certainty in the other world. Its ideas scarcely rise above temporal things. But the book of Wisdom underlines the spiritual aspect of the pains incurred by those who despise it. "Alas, the long tally of their sins! Trembling they shall come forward and the record of their misdeeds shall rise up to confront them . . ." They shall be seized with a terrible fear (Wisdom 4. 20; 5. 2). Their sins are "before the Lord", who will punish them with "fire and worm" (Ecclus. 17. 20). This fire, strictly speaking, denotes the devastations wrought by war and other disasters. The worm suggests the decay of the flesh and symbolizes the torments man suffers. All these plagues signify in many places the wrath of God, "that burns down to the depths of the abyss" (Deut. 32. 22).

However, the inspired authors of the Old Testament do

3 A. Gélin, P.S.S., *The Religion of Israel*, in this series, pp. 90-101.

not speak with any precision about these flames of Sheol, which manifest the wrath of God. To obtain more light on them, we must wait for the message of Christ. After him, it is the Church which expounds ever more clearly the words of Jesus who, by the sending of his Spirit, leads it into all truth. The furnace will never be extinguished: so the Church teaches. The lost will never escape from it.

The New Testament

The Master effects a gentle transition from his people's views to his own. He keeps the image of Sheol, the abode of the dead, who are "a prey to torments". There the wicked rich man endures the torture of heat and thirst. In vain he beseeches Abraham to release him: "There is a great gulf fixed between us and you, so that there is no passing from our side of it to you, no crossing over to us from yours" (Luke 16. 23-7).

There is, then, a sort of cliff, with no escape for those who are thrown down it. It is not Hades or the "region under the earth", whence the risen Christ comes forth with all his elect (Acts 2. 31-2: Eph. 4. 8-9). No; this sinister place does not yield up its victims. It is a "gehenna", a valley like the Vale of Ben-hinnom, spoken of by Jeremias, where the corpses were burned (Jer. 7. 31-2).

The Vale of Hinnom formed a ravine to the west of Jerusalem. There worship had once been paid to "Melek", which means "king", and is rendered "Moloch" in the Greek Septuagint. This idol demanded victims, and chiefly children. The fire devoured them; it was a charnel-house. To our Lord it represents the place of reprobation, the abode of the damned. It is also the abode of the demons; the kingdom of Satan, whose machinations will never be able to overthrow the kingdom of Christ (the "gates of hell"). It is the city of evil (Matt. 25. 41; 2 Peter 2. 4).[4]

Gehenna, also called hell, remains a place of perdition or extermination, as the Old Testament had already declared (Job 36. 6; Prov. 15. 11; 27. 20; Ps. 87. 12). There the accursed suffer the "second death" in tortures and terror (Apoc. 9. 2; 20. 14; 14. 11; Luke 16. 23-5: Acts 2. 24). "There will be weeping and gnashing of teeth" (Matt. 8. 12; 13. 42, 50; 22. 13; 24; 51; 25. 30). There will prevail the outer darkness, like dense clouds of smoke rising from a furnace of fire (Matt. 8. 12; 22. 13; 25. 30; 2 Peter 2. 4; Apoc. 9. 2; Mark 9. 42).

This fire, as Christ forcefully assures us, will endure for ever; it will be unquenchable (Matt. 3. 12; 25.41; Mark 9. 43, 47). Those who fall a prey to it will be, as it were, "salted", the Lord declares (Mark 9. 48). The damned will be "cooked" but never consumed. This undying hearth is for ever being replenished.

But while these instruments of torture never cease to act, Christ never says in explicit terms that those who undergo them will not be able to escape from them one day. The hypocrites, the causers of scandal, the egoists, all those, in a word, whom the judge condemns—will their sufferings be eternal? Will their expiation have no end? The Church, which alone possesses the full meaning of the words of her Lord and Master, in this case interprets them in their full rigour. For the damned, all is absolutely over. "Abandon hope, all ye who enter here . . . !"

The Fathers

Nevertheless, the Church hesitated and allowed its ideas to mature before finally pronouncing on the eternity of hell. Several Fathers believed that at the consummation of the ages

[4]Contrary to what has often been asserted, Gehenna (ge-hinnom) does not seem to have become a common incinerator for sewage.

Christ would restore all things in their original beatitude and would triumph over all evil. The end would match the beginning, and there would be no more lost souls.

It was in virtue of the universal restoration by our Saviour that a number of authors put forward this opinion. They appealed to the "recapitulation" of the universe in Christ, to the salvation of all men (the "apocatastasis"). St Paul had written: "Full completion comes after that, when he places his kingship in the hands of God, his Father, having first dispossessed every other sort of rule, authority and power; his reign, as we know, must continue until he has put all his enemies under his feet, and the last of those enemies to be dispossessed is death" (1 Cor. 15. 24-6). Origen used and misused this passage in order to construct his favourite theory, the return of the final realities to their beginning, to their first happiness:

> The end of the world and the consummation will come when sinners have fully undergone a punishment proportionate to their crimes . . . We believe that the goodness of God, through the mediation of Christ, will restore all creation to unity in the end . . . When all his enemies are subjected to Christ, when the last of them, death, is destroyed . . . , that will be the end: and that end enables us to imagine the beginning. In fact, the end always resembles the beginning.[5]

The Church did not follow Origen. But some authors, influenced in spite of themselves by the prestige of this genius and by a kind of Platonism (as in the school of Alexandria), adopted the idea of the full recapitulation as an hypothesis. Instigated by St Epiphanius, who could not endure Origenism, St Jerome vigorously opposed this system. But in spite of his war-cries, he still admitted that at least all the faithful, if not all men, would finally be saved; that the penalties of ordinary sinners would not last for ever, and that the sufferings even of the

[5] *De Principiis*, 1.6.

demons would be mitigated. Satan alone would never find redemption, contrary to Origen's opinion.[6]

Jerome's views on the salvation of the faithful and of sinners were preached by St Ambrose in his turn, and the two Gregories—of Nyssa and of Nazianzus—were convinced that at the end of the world everything would be re-established in the grace of the primal morning. There would be no more night. The earth would be saved. Those now plunged in vice would recover their primitive state. God would deliver them, and St Gregory of Nyssa went so far as to say that God would "heal even the author of vice, the devil".[7]

The idea of universal recapitulation also appealed to St Jerome. At the end of time, he wrote, Christ will destroy all evil and reconcile all things, so that all impurities will come to an end.[8] Many of the Fathers, then, favoured a final reconciliation of the universe with its Creator. Several of them held that Christians, who are signed with the blood of the Lamb in baptism, will some day be delivered from Satan's prisons. The faithful, at least all those who have performed a work of mercy, will find mercy with God. That is the opinion of some, but St John Chrysostom and, later, the greatest Doctors of East and West, Cyril of Alexandria and Augustine of Hippo, would never subscribe to the views of the "merciful". There is no deliverance from hell. Condemnation is perpetual.

It was this doctrine which prevailed in the Church. The weight of their authority tipped the scales for good to the side of eternal damnation. At most, and rather grudgingly, St Augustine was prepared to grant a sort of "pause" in favour of the damned: a temporary mitigation of the pains they have to endure. In this way he hopes to safeguard God's

[6]Migne, *Patrologia Graeca*, 7, col. 1256.

[7]*Oratio Catechetica*, 7-9; 14-15. (ed. Srawley, Cambridge, 1903.)

[8]*Contra Ioannem Hierosolomitanum*, (Migne, *Patrologia Latina*, 23, 368). St Jerome had originally been an "Origenist".

pity and the efficacy of the prayers said by the living for their dead.[9] But whatever the modifications and the nature of the sufferings to be endured, Augustine holds more firmly than ever to their eternity. "It matters little", he writes, "what is the nature of the penalty signified by the words 'worm' and 'fire', for if the one dies not nor is the other quenched, they are declared to be without end".[10]

St Augustine readily agrees that there are some who reject the physical reality of hell fire, but for his part he professes it.[11] This was also the opinion of Gregory the Great, whereas St Ambrose decided for the existence of a purely spiritual trial.[12] From the beginning, in fact, opinions were divided, some being inclined to take the texts literally, others interpreting the worms and flames in a wider and more analogical sense.

St Ignatius of Antioch declared that the martyrs escaped eternal fire by virtue of the fire of their sufferings. We find an analogous idea in the Acts of St Polycarp.[13] Minucius Felix, Tertullian and St Cyprian revel in descriptions of this river of fire which devours without consuming, because, they say, it is "intelligent". Clement of Alexandria, Origen, Gregory of Nyssa and Gregory Nazianzen are opposed to the material nature of hell-fire. The first two see it as the fever and fermentation of evil. Conscience will be tortured by its own pricks: anger, remorse and madness will harry it without mercy.[14] As for Jerome, he records Origen's opinion without denouncing it, as if, for once in a way, it met with his approval![15]

[9] *City of God*, XXI, II, 24. (In Healey's translation, XVII, 24)

[10] *Enchiridion*, 112. In Latin, *Qualiscumque poena significata sit nomine vermis atque ignis, certe si non morietur nec exstinguetur, sine fine praedicta est.*

[11] *City of God*, XXI, 10, 1 (In Healy's translation, XVII, 9 & 10).

[12] Ambrose, *Expositio sec. Lucam*, VII, 204.

[13] *Adv. Magn.* V.1: *Act. Polyc.*, II, 3.

[14] Origen, *De Principiis*, II, X, 4-5.

[15] *In Isaiam comment.*, XVIII (Migne, *P.L.* 24, 676).

One point must be noted. It must never be forgotten that the
Christians of the first centuries practically never considered
the condition of souls separated from the body. There is no
doubt that most of the Fathers of the Church taught that men's
fates were decided at their death. Some will be lost, the rest
will be saved. But in their view it is after the last judgement
and the universal resurrection that some will go into hell and
the others will see God in paradise. It was to the credit of
St Gregory the Great that he decided clearly for the position
that souls at their death immediately entered the place
destined for them. This conviction was ratified by the Church.
Moreover she is sure that God, who wills all men to be saved,
will help the heathen also to save themselves from the worm
and fire of hell.[16]

The theology of hell

That hell exists and is endless is a dogma of the Catholic
faith. And it would be useless to claim with, apparently,
Abbé Mugnier, that no human being is to be found there.
"Those who have done evil will go into everlasting fire",
declares the Creed attributed to St Athanasius (fifth century),
and the Second Council of Constantinople anathematizes any
man who says that "the punishment of the demons or of
wicked men is temporary".[17] This canon is no doubt aimed at
Origenism, at its concept of the reintegration of the demons
and the lost. It is nonetheless certain that the definitions of the
Church's Magisterium presuppose the presence of human
beings in hell.

The pains of hell never end: that is all that is of faith. True;
but in fact will any men be obliged to suffer them? It would

[16]St Augustine would have damned all heathens indiscriminately, but
in this he was not followed.
[17]Denzinger, *Enchiridion Symbolorum*, 40, 211. Cf. also the Fourth
Council of the Lateran, *ibid.*, 429.

be temerarious to deny it. It is at the least a certitude, and so is the existence of a torture called the pain of sense, (*poena sensus*), which is something additional to the pain of loss, or the absence of God.

Is hell a place? This is not a matter of faith. That it is a state of soul, a misery, an eternal torture, is what the Church imposes and presents as revealed truth. Certainly the Catholic can scarcely deny the existence of a "place", impossible though it is to "localize" damnation, which is primarily a spiritual situation, as we have already said about heaven. It is truer to say that one *is* heaven or hell, rather than that one goes there or enters it.

What, then, is this situation, this state of the lost soul? It is to be deprived of the vision of God: never to see the splendour of God's face. And that face is Love, Love in its infinity. This privation of God, of Love, is called precisely the pain of *loss*. That it makes men incapable of loving is an evident consequence. The absence of God leads to the disappearance of Love, inasmuch as sin consists in the radical refusal to love: to love God and in him to love one's brethren. The sinner loves himself, cut off from them, without them against them. The country priest of Bernanos' famous novel rightly exclaims: "Hell is not to love any more, Madame, not to love any more . . . The sorrow, the unutterable sorrow of these charred stones which once were men, is that they have nothing more to be shared."[18]

An excellent theologian writes that hell "is the land of dispersion and solitude. Hell is the antithesis of the communion of saints."[19] Solitude and emptiness carved out of the soul by estrangement from God.

"A second death", the Fathers and theologians call it, a sort

[18]*Diary of a Country Priest*, trans. P. Morris (London, 1937), p. 177.

[19]H. Rondet, S.J. *Un seul corps. Un seul esprit. La communion des saints* (Paris, 1952), p. 10.

of "living death".[20] It separates from all that gives meaning to life. It compels a definitive, total parting. It makes a break with the divine and the human. It plunges man into black, starless night. If there is light, it is that of the burning fire. In its glow, the damned soul perceives its ruin. It is abandoned by the God whom it has itself repulsed. And it realizes what it is losing; infinite beauty and love, united to procure it an eternity of bliss. It desires this God whom it can no longer help hating. Its heart is torn and crushed, perpetually tormented with this knowledge.

To this torment, compounded of remorse and despair, must be added the pain called the pain of *sense*. What is this pain? It is difficult to describe. The point at issue is a "fire". The term, we know, comes from the Scriptures. But these speak also of the gnawing "worms". These worms are a metaphor, as the theologians vie with one another in pointing out: an image of the soul which gnaws itself. Similarly, can we not see in the flames of Gehenna the symbol of a moral torture? The soul, eternally accursed, for ever consumes itself. St Jerome recognizes that many interpret the fire in this metaphorical sense, and does not say they are wrong. Even today none could blame them, for the Church has not defined the nature of this furnace. How can we explain the trial of fire?

St Thomas and his disciples put forward the hypothesis of constraint and imprisonment. The lost soul feels itself shut up in a sort of strait-jacket, strangled and always suffocating.[21] The advantage of this idea is that it corresponds to the structure of sin. The sinner has turned away from his sovereign Lord and preferred the lusts of this world. Aversion from God is met by his absence. Abuse of earthly things is met by their revenge. The creature, preferred before God, has become the soul's prison. "Things" have turned against the man who

[20]A. D. Sertillanges, O.P., *Les Fins humaines* (Montreal, 1946), pp.70-2.
[21]*Summa Theol., Supplem.*, Qu. 70, art. 4.

has failed to use them as a springboard whence to mount to God—which is what they were for. Their revenge is that they change their appearance. God's mirrors deprived of God, they are now disfigured and hideous. They have become spectres, haunting the souls of the damned. Caught in an infernal circle, the burning soul struggles in all directions against a wall of fire. Monstrous faces pursue him: the vision of a distorted world. Even this description must be moderate, for it does not pierce the mystery of the fire and does not come near discerning it. To exaggerate the visual picture of these terrors, like the medieval artists and old-fashioned preachers, would be to fall into a myth-form. Hell is no myth.

Anxious to avoid over-colourful images, Fr Rondet recently undertook to present the theological explanations of the pain of sense in modern language. It is "the expression of the pain of loss". Shall we say, it is not simply its translation, it seems to be rather its complement. It is to the pain of loss what the body is to the soul, what matter is to form. In heaven the elect have interiorized God's work of creation. It is to them and for them as it is to God and for God. But the damned must despair of this synthesis.

This explanation certainly does not offer much light to the mind. We give it for what it is worth. Who could dare to try to understand a mystery? Whatever may be this burning from which the soul suffers, it will one day extend to the body, in the universal resurrection. Till then, the soul alone endures a "physical" pain. "One who has had a limb amputated", writes Sertillanges, "really suffers pain from his absent limb . . . Why should a soul not suffer, physically in some way, once it has been separated from its body?"[22]

In all ages there have been Catholics who wondered whether the pains of hell exclude all possibility of relief. Even St

[22] *Les Fins humaines*, pp. 76-7.

Augustine, that stern doctor of grace, did not reject the idea. Peter Lombard appeals to him for a suggestion that through the prayers of the living certain lost souls suffer more bearable pains. St Thomas considers such an idea vain, unreasonable and presumptuous. He allows for some exceptional relaxation of rigour, some relief due to the prayers of a Christian. Commenting on this passage of his master, Sertillanges ponders this question:

> Must the law always be the law? I mean, are there not possible exceptions to this law, some restrictions which, without affecting the law itself, might evade its effect, in virtue of the divine mercies and for the comfort of so many souls, to appease so many others who are shocked and scandalized at such a possibility for our fellow-men?
>
> [. . .] In the Middle Ages stories were told of lost souls being freed from hell at the prayer of the saints. These stories were not very well authenticated, but that matters little. What I recall is that St. Thomas, when relating these events, did not declare them fictitious, which he would not have failed to do if they had been certainly opposed to doctrine. He simply says: "No doubt the destiny of these lost souls had not been really settled." God was able to make them be born again, in the manner of Lazarus, and thus to give them a chance to amend.
>
> [. . .] This is not the only possible hypothesis we might form, I mean within the doctrine we have to respect. God need not raise up a dead man in order to restore his chances of salvation. Here or elsewhere, he can reopen the opportunities of grace. What can stop him? The Law? He is its master. Even a human legislator, after laying down principles, reserves the power to judge of their application. In principle, hell is eternal. But with regard to any particular person, whoever he may be, no one can restrict the creator's freedom. God will do what he wills, as often as he will. As to this, we have no revelation.[23]

This long and carefully guarded passage from Fr Sertillanges

[23]*Les Fins humaines*, pp. 87-8.

has been worth quoting at length, for it shows that we must avoid all simplification on the problem of the mitigation of eternal punishment. Elsewhere, again on this question of remissions and degrees in the matter of damnation, he writes: "If the supreme misery of some lost souls is, as Dante says, that they have no hope of dying, we may believe that others, less completely disinherited, cling despite all to existence. It is the slender thread which still holds these eternal exiles to that which we love."[24]

The angelic Doctor writes with supreme assurance that to exist is a good. And it would be absurd to suppose that St Thomas places himself only at the point of view of abstract being (the ontological). To him, existence is always a free gift, a grace. And although the misery of damnation surpasses all imagining, it does not absolutely exclude the divine pity. The good deeds done by the lost in their life are still theirs. The lost are stamped with the malice which marked them at the moment of their death, but this malice is relative to each. None of them, unhappily, has willed to renounce it. But all were not equally guilty. Their activities, their virtuous tendencies plead for them. They do not intend to renounce them either. That is why the pain of sense varies in different cases.[25]

The gentle Abbé Emery used to say that the sufferings of hell were progressively diminished. Fr Hugueny opened the doors still wider and would finally send almost everyone to paradise. The Jesuit Fr Billot was scandalized at the "merciful" Dominican. It was in fact rather temerarious to make the lot of the damned endurable. It must never be forgotten that the

[24]*Catéchisme des incroyants*, vol. II (Paris, 1940), p. 198.

[25]De Brandt, *Christelijke eschatologie*, pp. 157-9. This excellent theologian admits the existence of a certain "well-being" in hell, in view of the relativity of eternal sufferings. At the Vatican Council, Cardinal Dechamps archbishop of Malines, refused to condemn those who admitted a mitigation of the pain of sense in hell. Cf. M. Becqué, C.SS.R., *Le Cardinal Dechamps*, vol. II, Louvain, 1956, p. 165.

dogma of hell springs from the divine justice, which must be feared if men are to love him better.

When God the Father sent his Son to die for us on the cross, it was not to deliver us from some milk-and-water hell.

PURGATORY

Reason is not capable of demonstrating that there must be, or is, an eternal punishment in the next life. At most it can perceive that the belief has good grounds. It has no more than a glimmer of light on the subject. Nor does critical and scientific study of the sources of faith procure absolute certitude. It is necessary for the Church to make a pronouncement, if the fact and the sense of an utterance of God are to be perfectly guaranteed. The Church does not only conform to revelation; it conveys it, it is one of its constitutive and vital elements.[26]

It is the Church, then, which has finally declared that there exists in the future life a never-ending punitive sanction, and that this is a revealed truth. The lost will be lost eternally, at least so far as God has declared in general.[27] But if the Church's Magisterium has defined that damnation is eternal, it has been careful to make clear that there are other sufferings to be endured after death which will not last for ever. This "hell", from which the Fathers say we shall emerge, it calls purgatory. The first Protestants accepted neither hell nor purgatory. Others, on the contrary, made hell into a purgatory, that is, a temporary expiation. That was as far as they would go. On the other hand, the Church, which holds the keys of

[26]De Brandt, *op. cit.*, pp. 97-9.

[27]Benedict XII added a reservation (*secundum Dei ordinationem communem*, according to God's ordinary design) to the dogma of eternal damnation because, according to a statement attributed to St John Damascene, Trajan was saved from hell through the prayers of St Gregory the Great.

revelation, affirms positively that divine justice has decreed two kinds of fire: the fire which devours and engulfs, which burns without ceasing, and the fire which mortifies and purifies, strengthens and heals. Fundamentally, purgatory is not so much a fire of torment as a "fire of joy".

St Catherine of Genoa, who is considered a specialist on the doctrine of purgatory, describes its sweetness as much as its pain: "I do not believe that it is possible to find a contentment to compare with that of the souls in purgatory, unless it be the contentment of the saints in paradise. This contentment increases daily through the influx of God into those souls, and this influx increases in proportion as the impediment is consumed and worn away."[28]

Purgatory is a time of maturing. "O blessed purgatory!" exclaimed a dying man. Thus it partakes in some of the beatitude of the elect as well as in the affliction of the damned. It has been compared to "a hell where they are happy and a heaven where they suffer".

To one who is in a state of grace this earthly life already brings a real happiness. In purgatory this happiness develops and is transformed, from the fact that the fullness of God is drawing near and its attainment is now certain. Evidently, there is also suffering in the state of these souls, separated from their bodies, and needing to be cleansed from some venial sins. The suffering involved in such an expiation in the other world is inexpressible. It has scarcely a common ground of comparison with the torments of this life, and so in a sense it surpasses them.

Pain and joy exist together in these souls who are undergoing a time of purification before entering paradise. This "time" must not be understood literally. Strictly speaking there are no days or hours in the life to come. It is a matter of progress, of development, a "spiritual time", in Jean Guitton's words, a

[28]Quotation from Fr Faber, *All for Jesus* (London, 1854), p. 359.

matter of quality, not quantity.[29] After all, these souls who are waiting for God see him better than they did on earth and are aspiring to contemplate him in the full light of the beatific vision. They are happy at being saved, unhappy at being held back and having to delay. Freed from the burden of matter, they are, as Guitton says again, "all to God, all in God, all for God".[30]

There exists, then, an intermediate state between the bliss of the beatific vision and the misery of damnation, a state of purification and expiation, so that the guilty actions of a man's life may be completely effaced after death. That is a dogma, which no Catholic can question. There are some young Christians who, in a spirit of generosity and community, prefer a religion without wages and rewards. True community is founded in the body of Christ. This body, which is Christ living and glorious in his Church, is before all else an "eschatological reality", as Fr Bouyer so rightly says. And that means a heavenly reality, a sharing in the unseen world, an enclave in this world of a country which lies on the far side of the border. The souls who have died in sanctifying grace, in the peace of the Lord, are members of this new people, this world which is coming and has already arrived.[31] Hence arises this contact between the living and the dead, or rather between those who are living in the world and those souls who live on the far side: who live more fully, while expiating in purgatory. They too form part, even more than we, of the one mystical

[29] *Réflexions sur le purgatoire*, in *Le Purgatoire, profond mystère*, bibl. *Ecclesia* (Paris, 1957), pp. 23-8, 26.

[30] *Ibid.*, p. 27.

[31] Bouyer is quoted by E. Van der Meersch, S.J., in *Le Purgatoire, profond mystère. Le Purgatoire dans l'Église*, pp. 29-34; 33. He notes: "The best of them find it difficult to understand this dogma, which only concerns each one's remote fate, whereas their ideal urges them to a Christianity which scorns every alibi and wants to be enrolled in the present fact of a community life" (p. 30).

body of our Lord, and the Church has always desired the faithful to pray for these elect souls "in suspense", who are waiting and ripening, and whose effective election depends on these prayers.

There has been prayer for the departed from time immemorial. The Jews themselves practised it in the second century before Christ. But only God knows how long they took to understand the immortality of the soul and the existence of penalties in the other world.

About 165 B.C., when King Antiochus Epiphanes of Syria tried to hellenize Palestine, the Jews, led by the Machabees, rose in revolt. Many of them were killed. Judas Machabeus at once asked for prayers. He and his followers felt sure that these fallen heroes would share in the resurrection, although several of them had retained looted objects of an idolatrous nature. In the second book of Machabees we read:

> Then he would have contribution made: a sum of twelve thousand silver pieces he levied, and sent it to Jerusalem, to have sacrifice made there for the guilt of their dead companions. Was not this well done and piously? Here was a man kept the resurrection ever in mind; he had done fondly and foolishly indeed, to pray for the dead, if these might rise no more, that once were fallen! And these had made a godly end; could he doubt, a rich recompense awaited them? A holy and wholesome thought it is to pray for the dead, for their guilt's undoing. (2 Mach.12. 41-6.)

This passage of Scripture is used in the liturgy of the dead, and is often quoted as a basis of the doctrine of purgatory. Still, it does not give us any precise information on the fate of those departed who need our prayers and sacrifices. We require other passages of the Bible, which at least allude to the destiny of those souls who are waiting for God. They say that he will judge and purify them by fire (Isaias 66. 15; Joel 2.3; 2 Thess. 1.8, etc.). Fire has often been connected with the ideas of justice and purity. It cicatrizes, cauterizes, disinfects.

It makes reparation. Was it not of this reparation that Christ was thinking when he gave the example of a man who could not get out of prison till he had disgorged and made restitution to "the last farthing"? (Matt. 5. 25-6). There are some, he said on another occasion, whose debts, that is, their faults, will find "no forgiveness, either in this world or in the world to come" (Matt. 12. 31-2). Thus, though the Master does not say so expressly, there are sins which *can* be forgiven in the world to come, as in the present.

More explicit, though very brief, is St Paul's passing reference to the case of the man who can only be saved "by passing through fire". The apostle is evidently thinking of the fire of the last judgement. He speaks too of "the day of the Lord that will disclose it, since that day is to reveal it in fire, and fire will test the quality of each man's workmanship" (1 Cor. 3. 10-15). Consequently, to see the pains of purgatory in these flames which test men would be to fall into a facile exegesis, to go too fast, to lose sight of the cast of mind of the early Christians. We must remember that above all else they hoped for the return of the risen Christ; that they waited for the final and universal resurrection which would bestow perfect beatitude on the people of God.[32]

Impressed by the attitude of the early Christians, John XXII, the last Avignon pope, denied one day in a famous sermon that the faithful could enjoy the beatific vision immediately after death, even if they had no sins for which to make expiation. Benedict XII followed another point of view. (His predecessor's opinion had not, incidentally, involved papal infallibility, as the necessary conditions were not present.) But John XXII had shown that he was not willing to cast the viewpoint of primitive Christianity lightly aside. Was he wrong to emphasize and honour the hope of the

[32] It must not be forgotten that the first Christians were more concerned than we with "the collective salvation of mankind".

Parousia when the truly resurrected, that is the elect, would be gathered around their glorious King at the table of the eternal banquet?

Gradually Christians came to see that the day of the Coming would not dawn so soon. They reflected on what we might call the "entr'acte" or the interval. (What, after all, are a million centuries to God?) How is it with souls after death? Where are they? What happens to them? Do they already experience the effects of a judgement? Do they enjoy beatitude before being reanimated with their bodies? All these questions gradually came to be answered, and they were cleared up more rapidly in the West than in the East.

At Lyons (1245) and Florence (1439) the Easterns approved of prayers for the dead. But they by no means supported the western Fathers in their exposition of the pains of purification. One of their own, Cyril of Jerusalem, had once declared that to offer a sacrifice in memory of the "saints" (in other words of Christians) was useful. There are some who die in the peace of Christ without being at once introduced to the heavenly country. They are waiting. This waiting, the Fathers say, constitutes purgatory, a temporary "exile" where the fire purifies, and because it purifies, it judges.

So says St Augustine, and likewise one of his disciples, St Caesarius of Arles. The fire devours what is bad and has not been atoned for by suffering on earth. It is rather a baptism, cleansing the soul for a last time, than a sort of torture which it must endure. It both consumes and consummates: it consumes the last impurities, consummates the joys of the spirit, of love. Quoting the famous lay theologian Von Hügel, Jean Guitton rightly remarks that "purgatory is the place not only of a debt . . . but of a metamorphosis . . ." The future life begins, in fact, in this world. And this world which it transfigures is finally transfigured in the next. Purgatory presides over this transfiguration. It is "a continued education"

(Lord Halifax). It is "the delay of beatitude" (Poujet): the vision "in suspense", but already well and truly guaranteed, no longer in jeopardy.[33]

It would be wrong, in describing purgatory, to regard it from either a spatial or a temporal point of view. It is a situation and a moment, rather than a place or a slowing-down. There is spiritual movement towards God. Not that the soul still progresses in the strict sense or acquires merit after death. It accepts the fact that God is perfecting his work in it and that the last barriers are being removed.

Freed from the remains of sin, from all guilt, all debts, the soul will "soon" take flight and penetrate into the paradise of the heavenly banquet, there to see God face to face.

Catholic doctrine, then, is clear: there exists a purgatory, the Council of Trent declares (Session XXV), in which souls are detained, who can be helped by the prayers of the faithful and especially by the sacrifice of the altar.[34]

But never has the Church defined or attempted to define the existence of a "real fire" other than that of the interior purification of souls; any painful reality besides the absence of and longing for God, for the sight of him. It is therefore legitimate to deny the existence of these "external" flames in purgatory. This is not to be temerarious, still less to offend against faith, but simply to decline to follow a more or less respectable opinion. In this field it is always lawful to hold another opinion. And one must never try to be more strict than the Church, "more Catholic than the pope". These departed who are "waiting" at the gates of heaven enjoy the peace of the Lord and are at rest in him. So we pray in the Canon of the Mass: *in Christo quiescentibus*. The crucible through which they pass ensures that they have been thoroughly

[33]J. Guitton, "La Pensée catholique et la vie éternelle," in the *Revue de Paris*, 1959 (12), pp. 119-30; p. 127. Pertinent reflections on hell will also be found there, pp. 112-24.

[34]Denzinger, 983.

impregnated, and rids them of all dust, all dross, so that like a precious metal without alloy they may be presented before God with their real weight of gold.[35]

We pray for the souls in purgatory, but can they pray for us and for others? Not a few theologians have said that they could, especially since the Council of Trent; Suarez, for instance and later Bellarmine and Alphonsus of Liguori. Christian piety has thought the same for centuries. Besides, these souls are surely very near to God. Why should they not be able, "in process of paradise", to intercede for men? The Communion of Saints is the circulation of the blood which gives life, and is called grace, in all those who form the body of Christ. His body has become their body. They love each other and pray in him, who is their tabernacle.

LIMBO

In the words of St Teresa of Avila, "hell is the place where no one loves". The damned is precisely one who is excommunicated, whereas purgatory is a world where they love, and the souls there, being in possession of grace, form part of the Communion of Saints, they are the Church suffering. But what are we to think of those who die without baptism or without sins of their own?

There is first the question of unbaptized children, who have not been slain for our Lord's sake, like the Holy Innocents. Then there are those adults who, being deprived of the two baptisms, of water (the sacrament) and of blood (martyrdom), are mentally or morally like children. Those, for instance, who are insane or mentally defective, and certain minds,

[35] De Brandt, op.cit., pp.177-85; A. Michel, Les Fins dernières (Paris, 1937), pp.106-8. These two authors soften the rigours of the Middle Ages and set the Church's doctrine in its true light.

entirely untaught or poisoned. That prince of modern scholastic theologians, Cardinal Billot, maintained in a sensational article that in some regions there were many adults incapable of sinning. The number is immaterial. The question is, whether those who have committed no actual sin and are unable to make an act of love to God (the baptism of desire), can be saved without being baptized or being martyred in the name of Christ. Apart from a miracle or some exceptional act on God's part, these children or quasi-children are excluded from the beatific vision.[36]

Against the Pelagians, St Augustine insisted on this exclusion. He went so far as to say regretfully that these children were condemned to a real pain of hell, although the mildest of all.[37] The great medieval theologians disagreed with Augustine. Abelard, Peter Lombard and, especially, St Thomas Aquinas granted, certainly, that these unbaptized little ones are "in hell", being deprived of the beatific vision, but they do not suffer from this, seeing that the vision is beyond the capacities and needs of their natural condition. Suffering in the soul presupposes a positive lack: a human being is tortured by hunger or thirst, but not by a rather vague desire for the cool and living water which wells up in eternal life.

Now, unless and until a human being has attained a certain maturity of spirit, and sanctifying grace has given it a higher aspiration for the things of God, it can scarcely have an appetite for them. Its nature is not outside the supernatural order, but neither is it elevated to the divine life. This incapacity for experiencing God in the eternal vision face to face involves lack of appetite. In contrast with the damned, the souls we are here considering are not troubled by what they have never come to desire. And, as most theologians add, they do not

[36]A. Michel, *Enfants morts sans baptême* (Paris, 1954). The author admits the possibility of this exception, according to the theologians' adage, "the divine action is not tied to the sacraments".

[37]*Contra Julianum*, V. 44 (Migne, *P.L.* 44, col. 809).

suffer any outward torture. This sort of painless situation is called limbo, the borderland.

About this limbo, one thing is certain. There is, after all, a punishment there, for there is a privation; that is, of the beatific vision. These persons are punished, not in their persons, for they have committed no personal sin, but in their nature, because in them this nature is affected with a fault, the stain of original sin.

Of course, this pain does not pain them, if we may put it so. It is "objective", not subjective, not felt. But it would be erroneous to say that there is no penalty in this state we call limbo. That would be to contradict the declarations of the Church's Magisterium. Innocent III, John XXII and the Councils of Lyons and Florence have all defined that "the penalty of original sin is the absence of the beatific vision: that of actual sin is the suffering of the eternal gehenna".[38] It is only this afflictive penalty which does not apply to unbaptized children. As to the absence of the vision, the defect resulting from this privation does not make them positively unhappy, as we have already said. There is, then, a limit which the "merciful" party must never exceed.

In all ages, and especially in recent years, theologians have suggested hypotheses which would allow salvation, in the full sense, to children who die unbaptized, and would safeguard what is called the "salvific" will of God. The Redeemer does wish to redeem all men and to open to all, if possible, the gates of paradise. It is not the purpose of this study to explain how we can reconcile this divine will with the "scandalous" fact which, at first sight, seems opposed to it: the case of countless infants who die unbaptized. But as these hypotheses necessarily tend to reduce the importance of limbo, to empty it as it were, it will be as well to note them.

The existence of limbo itself is not a matter of faith, nor

[38]Denzinger, 410, 464, 493, 693.

even of theological certitude. It is a solution which, up to now, it has been necessary to adopt: a solution of a hypothetical nature.

There are theologians, then, who have spoken of a lack being made good, by the desire of the sacrament. Those who have charge of a soul incapable of making a properly human act can act in its name. That was Cajetan's opinion long ago, and in our days it has been championed by Fr Héris. As to the children of pagans, Abbé Michel and Fr Santos hold that if their parents are in good faith they could ensure their children's salvation by offering and dedicating them to the mysterious God who is the object of their worship. And, as Abbé Bondes has asked, could not the Church herself, as mother of souls, present this saving vow to Christ?

Finally, others think that in the hour of death, or perhaps at the day of judgement, the child, like the adult, has a kind of illumination which makes it able to pronounce for or against its Master and Lord. When the soul is separated from the body, it is bathed in a light which obliges it to decide, to choose its eternal destiny.

Whatever we may think of these theories, Pius XII noted, when reminding us that it is not permitted to delay baptism, that its urgency could not be lessened by certain opinions, devoid of solid foundation, on the fate of children who die unbaptized.[39]

This chapter, which has dwelt on the severity of the divine Judge, must be brought to a close. Certainly the wrath of God,

---

[39] *Acta Apostolicae Sedis*, 50 (1958). On the whole question, see the long article by Peter Gumpel, S.J., "Unbaptized Infants; may they be saved?" in the *Downside Review*, November, 1954, vol. 72, No. 230, pp. 342-458. A very complete bibliography is appended. Also by the same, "Unbaptized Infants; a Further Report", in the *Downside Review*, Autumn, 1955, vol. 73, No. 234, pp. 317-46. Also G. P. Dyer, "Limbo", in *Theological Studies*, vol. 19, 1958.

so often described in the Bible, is a fact. It falls on those who attempt to put themselves in his place and rob him of his glory. Strictly speaking, it is the sinner who brings it into action. He has himself refused the infinite love. He has only himself to blame, not his Creator. And so the severity of God is not in contradiction with his immeasurable pity. The fear of God must not degenerate into being afraid of God, into a distrust, a suspicion, sometimes even a morbid terror.

Just as the justice of the Lord is a sign, a proof, of his kindness, man's fear should be a proof of his love, "incorporated" into that love. Then it will also be joy.

CHAPTER VII

HEAVEN AND EARTH

"Will death open nothing? Will it close everything?" So Maurice Maeterlinck asked himself in *Bulles Bleues*, the charming book describing his childhood.

When his friend, the poet Charles Van Lerberghe, lay dying, he took Maeterlinck by the hand and "swore that he would do all he could to show himself in the other world, . . . to let us know that he still lived . . .". A little bitterly, Maeterlinck comments that, like many others who have made the same vow, Van Lerberghe never came back. "He now lives only in me. That is all one can know, . . . all one can hope, so far."[1]

This man, who had always lived close to death, who had been so obsessed by the other world, could have found the key of the "great gate" only in the hands of Christ. But, forsaking the faith of his fathers, he seemed to be satisfied with a sort of theosophy which could tell him no secrets. He is like so many others who are never free from the thought of death and the future life, and demand proofs, "signs", as our Lord called them. This accounts for the popularity of spiritualism, which tries to enter into touch with the other world, the world of spirits, of the dead. Mediums, table-turning, automatic writing, cause the dead to come, to speak or to write.

[1]Maeterlinck, *Bulles Bleues* (Paris, 1948), pp. 221, 231.

The Church condemns the practice of calling up the dead.[2] She no doubt allows the possibility of automatic writing and the influence of the subconscious, as studied by the parapsychologists. But she forbids us to call up spirits; in other words, to try to force them to show themselves, to make themselves heard or seen. These unhealthy practices are based on either fraud or demonism.

But while the Christian faith is opposed to spiritualist teaching, it does not by any means reject all communication between earth and heaven. On Mount Tabor, Jesus conversed with Moses and Elias. In him, indeed, the two worlds meet. He is the centre of the Communion of Saints. As all the sun's rays meet in it, so in Christ all Christians form but one body. So we must not unduly separate the two worlds, the two Churches, in theological terms. The Church Militant is doubly bound to the Church Triumphant, and to the Church Suffering in purgatory too. To separate them would be to deny the dogma of the Communion of Saints. It would be to forget that ever since the Incarnation heaven itself has, may we say, "landed" on earth.

Naturally, there is a great difference between the earthly condition and the heavenly, between sanctifying grace and the light of glory. But no theologian would dare assert that the beatific vision has no connection with the divine indwelling in the heart of the just. The presence of the Blessed Trinity in the

[2]Condemnation by the Holy Office, Aug. 4, 1856: again Oct. 4, 1917. It was probably because of Gabriel Marcel's preface, which mentions a "planchette" being consulted, that M. de Jouvenel's book, *Du diapason du ciel* (Paris, 1948), was put on the Index. But it is always lawful for a mother who has lost her son to believe that he is dictating her thoughts to her. It is forbidden by Canon Law for her to urge or force her son or a spirit to speak and intervene. But she may think herself urged in her subconscious. And to say that the unseen, whether angels or spirits, act on us or in us, like grace, is not to fall into magic. The Fathers of the Church said as much. In a book dealing with our relations with the other world it is as well to get these things clear.

soul prepares and disposes it for the blissful state of contemplation in heaven. It is its germ, its prediction. Though there is
separation between the living and the dead, yet points of
contact between them remain or are established. Through the
circulation of grace, through prayer, through our Lord
himself in whom all are one, this life and the next communicate
with each other, as the obverse and reverse of the same reality.
Heaven sends out its waves: it is for the receiving station to
pick them up. That station is the soul of the man who prays for
the dead and remembers them: he is joined to them in God,
and more particularly in his incarnate Son. At times, without
having asked or begged for it, some men have been granted
a heavenly apparition. Christ, our Lady and the saints can
overcome the inaccessibility which results from their glory,
and unveil their faces, let their voices be heard.

Of course, theology can scarcely succeed in explaining
apparitions and visions. Theologians may speak of borrowed
bodies, or of images produced in the eyes of the beholders.
Perhaps, more simply, these senses have been enabled to
extend or rather heighten their capacity for perception, by
virtue of a special, extraordinary grace. The cloud which hides
paradise, lost in the beginning of time, and which conceals
Jesus since his ascension, may be partially drawn aside and
reveal a corner of heaven to privileged souls. In every age the
mystics have caught a glimpse of its marvels.

Henceforth earth is so near heaven, earthly life is so caught
up in the stream of universal redemption, that it too, as the
Apostle says, groans and strains, like a little bird trying its
wings. It too hungers and thirsts after justice. "If creation is full
of expectancy, that is because it is waiting for the sons of God
to be made known . . . with a hope to look forward to; namely,
that nature in its turn will be set free from the tyranny of
corruption, to share in the glorious freedom of God's sons.

The whole of nature, as we know, groans in a common travail all the while" (Rom. 8. 19-22). This redemption of the cosmos, which Teilhard de Chardin was fond of stressing, was an idea familiar to the Fathers. In their eyes, death was not to be thought of as a sickle, cutting off the soul entirely from the world of men and breaking all ties with it. It is integrated into the movement of the created universe. According to Origen, all existence is marked by contraries: heaven-earth, light-darkness, heat-cold. "Death and life come to complete and crown the series of contraries on which the existence of a creature is based. All movement to the heights or the depths is at once birth and death to another life."[3]

In the day of the Lord the earth will not be abolished but transfigured: the earth, which bore witness to Christ in his death, will sing his glory and that of the elect, with new instruments and in new tones. The world will be for ever renewed, made one.[4]

[3]H. Cornelis, O.P., "Les Fondements cosmologiques de l'eschatologie d'Origène", in *Rev. des Sciences philosophiques et théologiques*, vol. 43, 1950, pp. 32-50, 201-47; pp. 236-7.

[4]Sertillanges, *Les Fins humaines*, pp. 127-8: "The dispersion of the worlds in the ether will no doubt be succeeded by a sublime unity, created under the sign of the Spirit."

SELECT BIBLIOGRAPHY

In this series:

BERGOUNIOUX, F.-M., O.F.M., and GOETZ, Joseph, S. J.: *Primitive [and Prehistoric] Religions*; DRIOTON, Etienne, CONTENAU, Georges, and DUCHESNE-GUILLEMIN, J.: *Religions of the Ancient East*; LEMAÎTRE, Solange: *Hinduism*; GÉLIN, Albert: *The Religion of Israel*.

ADAM, Karl: *The Spirit of Catholicism*, London and New York, Sheed and Ward, 1934.

BARTHÉLEMY, D., O.P., and MILIK, J. T.: *Discoveries in the Judaean Desert*, Oxford and New York, Oxford Univ. Press, 1955.

BELL, R.: *Introduction to the Qur'an*, Edinburgh, Clark, 1953.

CERFAUX, L.: *Christ in the Theology of St Paul* and *The Church in the Theology of St Paul*, London and New York, Nelson, 1959.

DANIÉLOU, J., S.J.: *The Lord of History*, translated by N. Abercrombie, London, Longmans, and Chicago, Regnery, 1958.

GARRIGOU-LAGRANGE, R., O.P.: *Life Everlasting*, St Louis, Herder, 1952.

GUARDINI, R.: *The Last Things*, London, Burns Oates, and New York, Pantheon, 1954.

PRAT, Fernand, S.J.: *The Theology of Saint Paul*, London, Burns Oates, and Westminster, Md, Newman, 1945.

SARTRE, J. P.: *Existentialism and Humanism*, London, Methuen, 1948.

SCHMIDT, A. M.: *Calvin*, London, Longmans, and New York, Harper, 1960.

SHEED, F. J.: *Theology and Sanity*, London and New York, Sheed and Ward, 1948.

SMITH, G. D. (Editor): *The Teaching of the Catholic Church*, London, Burns Oates, and New York, Macmillan, 1952.

TROISFONTAINES, R., S.J.: *Existentialism and Christian Thought*, translated by M. Jarrett-Kerr, London, Black, 1950.

ZAEHNER, R. C. (Editor): *The Concise Encyclopedia of Living Faiths*, London, Hutchinson, and New York, Hawthorn, 1959.

The Twentieth Century Encyclopedia of Catholicism

The number of each volume indicates its place in the over-all series and not the order of publication.

TWENTIETH CENTURY ENCYCLOPEDIA OF CATHOLICISM

All titles are subject to change.

6884   BL   2707
       535
      .B4213
       1960